L.A.G.I.

LIVING AS GOD INTENDED

7 Practical Steps to Uncovering &
Fulfilling Your Purpose in Life

By

Nathaniel Odin

Disclaimer: The purpose of this book is to provide a unique source of spiritual information and inspirational messages regarding personal development and living purposefully according to God's intended plan. It's not meant to replace professional counsel for legal, medical, or financial matters, or emotional or psychological issues. Referral to a qualified professional counselor is recommended for use outside the scope of this publication which is intended for general use and not as a specific course of treatment. Neither the author nor publisher takes any responsibility for loss occasioned to any person or organization acting or refraining from action as a result of information contained in this publication.

Unless otherwise indicated, Scripture is taken from The Holy Bible, New International Version®, NIV®, Copyright© 1973, 1978, 1984 by International Bible Society. Used by permission of Zondervan. All rights reserved.

For information, please write to:

Winners Chapel Int'l London Aka World Mission Agency

European Headquarters, Churchill Close,

Green Street Green Road, Dartford, Kent.

DA1 1QE

DEDICATION

This book is dedicated to God Almighty- my Creator and my Father.

"I will praise you because I am fearfully and wonderfully made; your works are wonderful, I know that fully well."
~ Psalm 139:14.

AND

To every individual who will read this book and decide to live a purposeful life as God intended for him or her.

TABLE OF CONTENT

INTRODUCTION

"Oh yes, you shaped me first inside, then out; you formed me in my mother's womb. I thank you, most High God, you are wonderful! Body and soul, I am marvelously made! I worship in adoration—what a creation! You know me inside and out; you know every bone in my body; you know exactly how I was made, bit by bit, how I was sculpted from nothing into something. Like an open book, you watched me grow from conception to birth; all the stages of my life were spread out before you, the days of my life all prepared before I'd even lived one day."

(Psalms 139:14-16 MSG)

When God made you, there was a purpose in His mind; there was a desire in His heart which can only be accomplished through you. This is the reason why He made you and sent you to the world. No man is walking on the surface of the earth without a purpose. Sadly, only a few people discover this purpose before leaving earth. Among those who discovered their divine purpose, only a few maximized and fulfilled it. This is not God's will for us. He has not planted so much in us just for the sheer purpose of it. Everything He has put in us is important to fulfill His intent for us.

The Creator had a clearly defined and unique design in mind when he decided to create you with all the intricate endowments that will certainly make you a winner in life. You are a divinely customized and purposefully built product, who went through heavenly quality control before you were released with the intent to take charge, be fruitful, multiply and replenish the earth that you might honor him.

Jesus Christ had a purpose on earth; He recognized it and lived His entire thirty-three years with this consciousness. At the age of twelve, He was found in the temple explaining the Scriptures to the teachers of the law. Everything He did propelled Him to the fulfillment of His purpose. He went about doing well because that was His reason for being on earth. Jesus was a man like us too, and he must have faced many of the things we are tempted with, but he remained sinless, given the sacredness of His calling. He kept up with the good works until He restored humanity to God, which is His purpose on earth.

The only reason why people go about living life as they want is that they do not know how unique they are. Many people are oblivious of the potentials hidden in them. They have not realized that there is more to life beyond going to college, getting a job, getting married, and going to rest at an old age. We all have been made to be instruments in God's hands and blessings to our world. To navigate the journey of life more successfully to reach your divine destiny, you must fully realize and fulfill your sacred calling and responsibility, which is God's intended vision and purpose for your life. You will never be able to live as God intended if you do not know why He has made you. It is the knowledge of your true identity that enlightens and determines how you live.

A princess grows up carrying herself as a future queen not only because she has been trained to be one but also because she looks into the mirror and sees a queen. She sees her beads and jewelry and adornments, and they all remind her of who she is. This knowledge then informs and fuels how she speaks, acts, and behaves. When you do look into the mirror, who do you see? Beyond the doctor or the teacher, what do you see yourself as?

There is a special gift in you that the world is waiting for, there are destinies tied to your testimonies, organizations and industries are waiting to benefit from your unique gifts. You are the solution to some people's problems. You are the answer to their prayers but do you even see yourself in this light? You are not an ordinary person; however, you will not become great by waiting, greatness is not by chance but by taking bold steps and taking advantage of life's opportunities. You have to first see yourself as God sees you before you can fulfill His intent for you. You can't carry out an assignment you do not know. You have to discover who you are first.

Even though many people live for decades, a good number of them never step into their purpose. They do not even know there is a purpose for them. A wise man once said, "The wealthiest place is the graveside." Yes, more gifts and potentials are lying fallow on tombs in the cemetery than there are in use among the living. Why is this so? There are many of us, for some reason, who never step into their purpose. A lot of people are merely chasing after the mundane things of the world. Too many people are satisfied with the status quo; there is no zeal for more. As long as there is food on their tables and they own a home to live in, they have no worries.

The greatest question a man or woman of purpose must answer is "Why am I on earth? Why was I given the privilege to be born?" Ask yourself what the purpose of your existence is. There has to be more to you. You weren't just born to add to the numbers. Why are you where you are in existence right now? What are you wired to manifest? What's your purpose? Look inward, not outward because uncovering and fulfilling your purpose in life is an inside job that comes with doing a lot of soul searching.

Many mistake their qualifications and career pursuit as a vision; some others have taken to ambition. There is a defined purpose to why you are on earth. Every manufacturer has a purpose in mind before a product is designed, tested, and released to the consumers. When a manufacturer designs a product, he must have first discovered a problem and designed that product to solve it. There is no product without a purpose.

You are the product while humanity and global content are the consumers; the manufacturer is God, our Creator. Psalm 100:3 makes it clear that we are not the ones who made ourselves. God made us, and if He did, He saw a need to. Jeremiah 1:5 says, *"Before I formed you in the womb, I knew you; before you were born, I set you apart, appointed you as a prophet to the nations."* This Scripture explains that God knew us before we even knew ourselves. He knew us and what we would be before we were conceived. Right before the beginning of our existence, He set us apart for a specific purpose, and it's our responsibility to discover this purpose and carry out His will on earth, as it is done in heaven.

The psalmist further declared in Psalms saying, "I am wonderful and fearfully made." The Message translation puts it this way: *"Oh yes, you shaped me first inside, then out; you formed me in my mother's womb. I thank you, most High God, you are wonderful! Body and soul, I am marvelously made! I worship in adoration—what a creation! You know me inside and out; you know every bone in my body; you know exactly how I was made, bit by bit, how I was sculpted from nothing into something. Like an open book, you watched me grow from conception to birth; all the stages of my life were spread out before you, the days of my life all prepared before I'd even lived one day."* (Psalm 139:14). Another translation, The Voice, brings more light: *"I will offer you my grateful heart, for I am your unique creation, filled with wonder and awe. You have approached even the smallest details with excellence; your works are wonderful; I carry this knowledge deep within my soul."*

You see from the above verses of the scriptures; it is clear that you were shaped, designed, formed, and created by God with excellent breathtaking details but complex beyond what any fellow creature can understand or explain. No man can help another man. We are all limited in the findings or discoveries of the intricate and complex nature of a human being. If you want to see yourself as you are, you need to ask God because He's the One who made you; and since he carefully and thoughtfully created you to be unique, it makes a whole lot of sense for you to understand the purpose behind the life He gave you in the first place.

You are so unique and filled with awesome characteristics, but until you discover them, you might not live your fullest life. You will pass through the earth just as you came, loaded to the brim, carrying these gifts to the graveyard where no one needs them. You need to wake up! You must die empty; you must give out everything God loaded you to bless the world with. Enough of the complacency! You need to wake up!

The enemy will do everything to distract you from seeing this picture that God did not hide from us but has presented for your discovery. He will try to make you satisfied with the transient things of this world which have no value. However, you need to know that only God can show you who you are. Apple cannot give you the finite details of a Samsung product.

Every manufacturer has a patent right to their product. The best of you that you know is only a hint of the best of you as designed by God. Every wise user of a product will consult their manual. As God's children, the manual of our destiny is God's word, printed in the form of a book called the Bible.

Give yourself to the study of God's Word; what does it say about you? If it calls you a king, why live like a slave. You need to build a strong relationship with your Father in heaven; He is the only One who can provide the sure roadmap for your life. It is only when you know what He wants for you that you can live out His intent. Speak to God; ask Him to show you who you are. Jeremiah 33:3 says, *"Call to me, and I will answer you and tell you great and unsearchable things you do not know."* When you speak to God, He will reveal to you every hidden thing.

"'For I know the plans I have for you', declares the Lord, 'plans to prosper you and not to harm you, plans to give you hope and a future. Then you will call on me and come and pray to me, and I will listen to you. You will seek me and find me when you seek me with all your heart.'" (Jeremiah 29:11-13). To discover God's plans for you, you need to seek Him. His Word assures us that He will hear us and give answers to our prayers.

However, you need to search within your spirit because your spirit is the part of you that communicates with God. God speaks to us spirit to spirit. 1 Corinthians 2:9-10 says, *"However, as it is written: 'What no eye has seen, what no ear has* *heard, and what no human mind has conceived – the things God has prepared for those who love Him – these are the things God has revealed to us by His Spirit. The **Spirit searches all things, even the deep things of God.***"

There is no man born without a purpose. There is no man sent on earth by God to merely live and die without making an impact on the earth. God has set each one of us apart for a peculiar purpose. Whether you're in your 20's, 30's or even 40's, it is not too late to discover your purpose. It is never too late to start living out God's intent for you. Look inside you; what gives you a sense of fulfillment? What are you passionate about? You need to identify your passions, your goals, and your values; but more importantly, what God is saying. You have to become intentional about how you live your life.

Quit belittling yourself. You are not an accident; God has a plan for you. This would apply to you even if you were conceived out of wedlock. You didn't just come by chance; you came to fulfill a purpose, and one of the greatest favors you will ever do yourself is to discover that purpose.

When you discover your true purpose on earth, your life finds meaning, and there will be the motivation behind the things you do. You are will not merely live life as it comes; rather, you will be deliberate about your decisions. Your steps will be calculated, and all of your energy will be geared in the direction of your vision. You only start living the moment you discover who you are.

In the words of Dr. Myles Munroe, "The greatest tragedy in life is not death; it is life, a life that fails to fulfill its purpose and potential." The world is waiting for you. We all can't wait to experience the version of greatness in you.

Enough of the complacency! Wake up today and take charge of your life! No one's going to live your life for you. You have your life in your hands. You need to start doing something tangible with it. It's not all about the cars, the houses, and fame; it's about God. You need to start living out His plan and purpose for you. It always starts with a decision. Wake up today!

For easy understanding and application, we have broken this book down into seven practical steps. As you read each chapter, it is advised that you make your notes out of them and then find practical ways to apply them in your daily life.

I strongly believe that this is one book that will change your life forever, I assure you.

Congratulations in advance.

Much Love,

Nathaniel Odin

CHAPTER ONE

STEP OUT

Step out of what?

You need to step out of your comfort zone. You need to wake up and decide to start living your life. A comfort zone is a place of ease and comfort; there's no pressure or desire for more. You are simply satisfied with what you're used to. When you're in your comfort zone, your brain doesn't want any alteration. Your body is relaxed, and it does not want to welcome any sort of change. And truthfully, we all love our comfort zone. We all want the comfort and peace of mind it brings.

However, no one ever remains in his comfort zone and becomes great. If you remain in your comfort zone, you will never move beyond your present level. You can't become who you want to be if you choose to remain where you've always been. Having discovered what God wants for you, you need to start taking action. Normally, you will be tempted to remain where you've always been. There's always a temptation to remain in a place you're familiar with than a place you're uncertain about. But if you will ever achieve anything, you need to leave the familiar for the unfamiliar.

In this day and age where our lives have become so cluttered with entertainment and other forms of engagements, it's very easy to want to remain in a comfort zone without any real vigor and passion for being and doing more in life. In as much as the comfort zone is a comfortable and convincing place that always makes us feel like that is where we are meant to be, it's where ambition goes to sleep, and where most of your dreams dissolve into a world of undiscovered potentials and possibilities.

Unfortunately, we are easily enticed by the comfort zone because we prefer the status quo instead of making bold moves to step out and achieve more. Until you step out, you will never see the reality of what is awaiting you. If the founder of Alibaba, Jack Ma, remained with his lecturing position, he would never end up as the richest man in China. He had an idea, and he stepped into it. Even though he had no previous experience, he stepped out to fulfill his purpose. While staying in your comfort zone can be stress-free and result in a steady performance, stepping out of your comfort zone is risky but hugely rewarding because the challenges that come from stepping outside of one's comfort zone usually creates the condition for peak performance – Like in the case of Jack Ma.

In truth, when you open yourself to vulnerability and possible stress and anxiety by stepping outside your comfort zone, your chances for great achievements and accomplishments are heightened due to the fact that the ability to take risks outside your comfort zone can lead to real personal growth and development. Your brain goes through a lot trying to adjust to a new pattern of life, but when it is trained, it becomes used to the newness. It is quite easy to resolve to the normal pattern of sleeping, waking, working, and going to bed. Bringing in something foreign like the pursuit of a passion may be alien to your body, and it is only natural for your body to react. Nevertheless, do not allow this reaction to stop you from pushing further. There is no point in discovering your purpose without attempting to fulfill it.

It was okay to live carelessly before the discovery of purpose; it was okay to do things the way you wanted, but now that you know what you are supposed to live for, you need to start taking steps and the first step to take is to leave your comfort zone. The comfort zone is sweet, but nothing ever grows there. You need to keep the things you find easy to do aside so you can start the seemingly difficult things because they are the actions capable of propelling your destiny. Remember nothing good comes easy, and to achieve personal greatness, you must be willing to go all out and meet life with passion and enthusiasm.

You don't have to pamper yourself and make excuses; excuses for your incapability, inconsistency, and laziness. Proverbs 22:13 (TLB) says, *"The lazy man is full of excuses. 'I can't go to work!' he says. 'If I go outside, I might meet a lion in the street and be killed.'"* I find this particular verse ridiculous, but that's the way many of us are. When it's time to get something done, we come up with ridiculous reasons why it can't be done. Sadly, the more excuses we make up, the more we miss out on what God is calling us to do. You need to wake the sleeping giant in you, rise from the bed of excuses and put your hands to work. Moreover, to gain greater rewards in life, you must never rest on your laurels.

Even though you don't enjoy the kind of life you want in your comfort zone, you choose to stay there because you're too lazy to start doing something. Your comfort zone will never let you see beyond now. As long as you are in your comfort zone, you have the temporary comfort you need, and aspiration for better things is seen as unnecessary stress. This is not your fault. It is the way every man is wired; evolutionary change always appears awkward to us at first, but once the feeling is overcome once and for all, we become undefeatable. As a Christian, I grew up hearing the phrase "from faith to faith, from glory to glory," meaning that the constant state of evolutionary change in our lives serves a great purpose, as it is eventually and ultimately transforming us into the individuals that we were designed and destined to be.

Life begins at the end of your comfort zone, yet we all never want to leave there. Being in your comfort zone reduces anxiety and fear. It is so easy to predict what will happen, unlike when you go out to try something new. You don't know what to expect. Your brain wants to save you all of the stress even though it's harmful to the fulfillment of your destiny. Yes, it's harmful to your destiny because remaining in such a predictable or repetitive life cycle that is comfortable for you will not help propel you to aspire for more in life. On the other hand, leaving your comfort zone might be uncomfortable at first. Still, if you continue to push yourself beyond its limits, you will eventually discover great things about your true potentials which will then help you to attain greatness.

Robin S. Sharma said, "As you move outside of your comfort zone, what was once unknown and frightening becomes your new normal." All you need at first is to step out. Damn the consequences. There was a time in my life here in the United Kingdom when I was without a legal document to work or continue with my studies; and being a believer, it was not an option to go the wrong way. On the other hand, it would be anti-scriptural to stay idle. I sat down, trying to reason my way out of the situation, and then decided to enroll in a college without letting them know I was an undergraduate student. While they saw me as one who needed support, it turned out that I became a support structure within that institution; it landed me a role I never applied for in the community of Portsmouth, doors for certificates were opened, and I successfully acquired knowledge and experience vital in my assignment today.

See the vision ahead of you and begin to work towards it. Your vision will never come to life if you merely cover it up in your mind. It can only be actualized when you start doing something. As a matter of fact, stepping out of your comfort zone requires you to broaden your vision and extend your personal boundaries in order to create a life that is both purposeful and fulfilling. So, think big and act big knowing that you have a big God who must surely see you through.

You have to choose between comfort and courage; you can't keep them both. You will either choose to wrap yourself up in comfort or settle with the cold and harsh realities of life. It is very difficult to leave your comfort zone, but you need to step out of comfort and take the risk to live the life you have been called to live. Your life will never change until your pattern of living changes. Before you can achieve anything, your comfort zone has to be disrupted. You have to be unkind to yourself at first if you want to live a fulfilling life now and peaceful life in your old age. So, how about some denial now in exchange for permanent enjoyment in the future? How about some discipline now just in order to put a smile on the Father's face? Choosing to stay in your comfort zone today will cost you your sense of fulfillment tomorrow.

It's so easy to remain in a place of comfort because no energy and discipline are required from us. Our laziness is justified, and we are allowed to come up with a thousand and one excuses. In short, the comfort zone is sweet! There's no pressure to do anything. I love my comfort zone - we all do — but if I choose to stay there, I'll have to stand shame-faced before the Lord on the Day of Judgment. That's too much to pay! I should stand boldly before my Father, confident that I have done what He required of me on earth. Don't be like Esau; don't settle for temporary enjoyment at the cost of your future!

It may be nice to sleep fifteen hours a day, to see a movie as often as you want to, or, even pile up all your work for "later". We all find it cool to idle around, chatting with our friends and having no tangible things to wrap our arms around. It's convenient to stay in a job where nobody forces you to think or carry out challenging tasks. Comfort is body-friendly but deadly to your spirit because it will kill your real you. In the end, you'll hate yourself; you'll watch others and wish you had done better; you'll wish you could turn back the hands of time, but it'll be too late.

You need to discipline your body if you want to really enjoy life. This is why Paul said, *"But like a boxer, I buffet my body {handle it roughly, discipline it by hardships} and subdue it..."* (1 Corinthians 9:27-AMP). If you want to live a life full of positive results, you need to discipline your body. As a matter of fact, your body is the first enemy you need to combat. You need to learn to say a firm NO to the cravings of your body. If you yield to all the desires of your body, you'll not only live an unfulfilled life; you will not be making the Father glad.

If you have to cut your hours of sleep, do so. If you have to move out of your circle, do so. If you have to stop enjoying some privileges, please do so. Take up another job if your present job isn't bringing out the best in you. Give yourself challenging tasks. Put yourself under deadlines. Start with denying yourself things that pull you away from fulfilling your purpose. Start keeping records of your little achievements knowing that when you pause to appreciate your little victories, more fortunate events will eventually unfold and lead you to become the best version of yourself. Surely being this intentional and daring in life isn't always a smooth sail. Still, as you pay attention to your small wins and take full responsibility for the related actions that brought them into being, you are essentially reminding yourself that 'I'm on the right path'. In truth, nothing lifts your spirit, builds your confidence, and gives you the boost you need to keep going like this kind of 'self-reminder' – which comes from leaving your comfort zone.

Having said that, leaving the comfort zone requires energy; it demands of us; it calls us into action. Without a proper drive, we will never be able to leave that place of comfort. We choose to stay where we've always known because we are not really sure we will get the life we want from doing the unknown. This was usually the case when you had tried leaving before but were faced with challenges. Common sense just tells you to stay. Common sense tells you the stress may not be worth it. But you know, common sense isn't always right. We can't rely on common sense. God's principles are always accurate. If you apply them, you will get the results attached to them.

Refusing to step out of your comfort zone is a sign of laziness. A vision-driven person has to be hardworking and zealous. Sadly, some people are never ready to commit themselves to anything. They are not ready to pay the price for greatness. Leaving your comfort zone will not be easy; it will take so much from you – dedication, commitment, and consistency. But when you decide to leave, you'll be glad you did.

The comfort zone is the greatest enemy of your destiny. You are at peace, but you can't boast of anything. Worse still, you cannot fulfill God's plan for you. When Jesus Christ left the city for the wilderness for forty days and nights, it wasn't easy for Him, but He had to be trained for His ministry. He could have chosen to sit back at home with his family, helping His Father at the shop, but He knew the weight of the responsibility upon Him. He knew what laziness and complacency would cost Him. The Bible told us He was hungry, and that was why He could be tempted with food. Yet, He did not yield because He knew what would be at stake. Jesus had to pay the price.

This is the attitude we need to portray in life. Discover the purpose of your existence and start doing something about it. No matter how tempting, deny yourself of anything that can stop you from fulfilling that purpose. Be the drive your body needs. Stop waiting for external motivation; you may never get it. Just sit down and count the cost. Identify the things you need to give up and those things you need to pick up. Eliminate the enemies; embrace the friends. Or better still, accentuate the positives and frustrate the negatives.

David was not like his other brothers. He was different. While most of his mates would have been playing around, he was busy tending to his Father's sheep in the bush. It was not a sweet experience because he was faced with dangerous animals that could have possibly killed him, but he was being trained all through the process. When he faced Goliath, he killed him like a rat.

The magnitude of your calling determines what would be demanded of you. The Bible tells us that much is expected from him to whom much has been given. You are not ordinary; you are not like any other person. You need to start living life with the consciousness of who are. You can't love your life and still have it. It is a principle in the kingdom. If you have your life, you will need to lose it first.

You cannot be complacent and still fulfill a purpose. You cannot be lazy and still fulfill your destiny. The demands are high, and you need to start training yourself for this. Cut your hours of sleep; pull out of unnecessary parties; reduce the hours spent in front of the TV. Let your vision begin to push you. The future you envision will not happen by chance. You have to start working towards it, and this begins by leaving your comfort zone. More than ever before, you have to be intentional about your life.

As God's children, we are even more rest-assured that God is on our side and He is helping us to be who He wants us to be. We know we are not riding on our strength only. Joshua 1:9 assures us: *"Have I not commanded you? Be strong and courageous. Do not be frightened, and do not be dismayed, for the Lord your God is with you wherever you go."* The One who has called you is faithful enough to keep you till the end. In your weakness, call on Him to strengthen you.

FEAR OF THE UNKNOWN

Sometimes, fear is a signal to pull us away from danger, but most times, it is an enemy that traps us on the spot. When we ought to move forward, fear holds us back under the assumption that we may be consumed. Virtually everyone nurses the fear of what they do not know. It is normal to be skeptical about something we have never tried before, but when subjected to fear of failing even before trying, we are robbed of everything beautiful the future holds. Fear of the unknown sends a warning where there's no danger. It keeps you from trying and blinds you with multiple reasons why it won't work. As writer Suzy Kassem says, "Fear kills dreams than failure ever will." Fear has caused many people to miss out on opportunities that would have enabled them to discover possibilities and reach their full potential.

The fear of the unknown is one of the greatest reasons why people never try. It is the reason why many people never fulfill God's purpose for them. It is the reason why many gifts and talents are wasting in the graveyard – they never tried; they were too scared to try. It is the reason why kings are living as slaves and chiefs as ordinary men. No wonder Jeff Mcclung boldly declared "Don't let the fear of the unknown keep you from experiencing a life greater than you have ever known."

The most influential people in the world today are not men without fears. They have fears and doubts. They have reasons never to try. But these men have learned not to be controlled by their fears. They are men who have learned to silence their fears and step out into the world of opportunities. They are men who have refused to be held down by their uncertainties. Moreover, one thing that these successful men and women have in common is that they have managed to overcome the oppressive and paralyzing effects of fear. It's not that they are not also afraid of the unknown, but they focus on the good that could be, and not on the bad that might be. They know that to become truly successful in anything, you have to be courageous and take action despite fear.

As thoughts of impossibilities are spurred, tackle them with thoughts of possibilities. When your mind tells you, "What if it doesn't work? What if they don't like you?" Answer with "What if it does work? What if I am accepted?" There are always two options, but you will never be able to tell which is for you until you have tried. You won't have anything to lose when you try. You'll only regret that you never tried.

Great people also have their fears, but they choose not to be controlled by fear but by the vision in their hearts. The more you step out of fear, the more you can conquer other fears. Much more, God's Word tells us that we have not received the spirit of fear, but of power, love, and a sound mind. This tells us that fear is not from God but from the devil. The devil presents us with logical reasons why we should never take a step. He feeds us with lies that where we are now is just good enough because he doesn't want us to fulfill God's purpose for us.

God's Word assures us that God is on our side. Proverbs 21:5 (ESV) says, *"The plans of the diligent man lead surely to abundance."* God's blessings are upon you; you cannot fail. Step out with this assurance; step out knowing that the end has already been taken care of from the very beginning.

You may nurse fears about trying because of past failures but trust me, this is not a good reason to stop trying. You need to trust God and the unique abilities He has kept in you. You need to believe in yourself. You need to trust yourself to be up to the task. Feed on God's Word and what it says about you. It helps to boost your self-confidence and how you perceive yourself. If you want to live for God, you need to see yourself through God's lens. If you see yourself as the devil sees you, you will evolve to be who he wants you to be.

In order to also build your confidence, you need to make yourself ready for the vision ahead of you. Commit to personal development; develop new skills; read books; get a mentor; make sure you're learning. Do all you can to be truly prepared for the future you envisage. Before Paul became a preacher, he was separated for many years. It was during this period that He had a series of encounters with God and Spirit-inspired revelations. His training in the secret fuelled his passion in an unexplainable way and helped him to stand out among other preachers.

When the devil whispers to you, tell yourself "I can do all things through Christ who strengthens me!" learning to tame your fears and stepping out into your vision will do you a lot of good. Seneca said, "We are frightened than hurt, and we suffer more from imagination than from reality." There's more we lose from not trying than we actually lose from trying.

Face your fears; if you don't, they'll keep mounting until you are completely consumed and too weak to try. The best way to conquer fear is to face it. In the end, you'll discover that what you had always feared was never even there.

Even though you may be afraid, step into your dreams. As you do, your fears will dissipate, and you will be drawn closer to the fulfillment of your purpose. William Shedd once said: "A ship is safe in harbor, but that's not what ships are for." Write down your vision today; set the goals on how to achieve them. Start doing something today. Procrastination is a killer of dreams. The more you postpone, the less passionate you become about your vision.

Remember; you were not made just to discover purpose. You were made to also fulfill it. Life in itself is neither a funfair nor a playground; life is a battlefield. Life is filled with challenges; until you confront them, you cannot conquer and come to the front…Step out!

CHAPTER TWO

STEP IN

The journey of a thousand miles, they say, begins with a step, however, just one step is not enough to discover your purpose; before your vision can be actualized, and you need to fully step into it. You must be ready to pay the price required for your vision to materialize. You must be ready to commit yourself to the actualization of your vision. Once you discover what you are wired for, don't hesitate to step into it and begin to function seamlessly. The discovery of purpose is the foundation upon which you build; it is your driving force. Bringing the vision (the picture of your God's intention) in your heart to life requires focus, hard work, and commitment.

Having left your comfort zone, you need to step into your vision. You did not step out of your comfort zone to get into another comfort zone. You stepped out to start doing what you have been called to do. However, only a foolish man sets out on a journey for which he is not prepared. The enthusiasm to be the version of yourself in your vision may be misleading. You need to calm down and strategize. Setting out without acquiring wisdom will lead to failure and give you a reason never to try again.

Here, I will be discussing five applicable steps you need to step into your vision. I call them the **DRPPR principle**. They include:

- Discover and understand your vision
- Rationalize your vision
- Pursue your vision
- Pay the price
- Remain consistent

DISCOVER AND UNDERSTAND YOUR VISION

Vision is the unfolding of God's plans for an individual, organization, or entity. Your vision is like traveling into time and knowing what the future holds for you. It's an image of your future reality that makes you feel excited and hopeful to the extent that you are willing to sacrifice for it. In short, it is the discovery of your vision that results in the recovery of your destiny. To step into your vision, you must first discover what you are designed to fulfill; that is to say, you must first have a clear understanding of what your purpose in life is, and this clear understanding is called the clarity of purpose. In the words of Napoleon Hill, author of 'Think and Grow Rich': "There is one quality that one must possess to win, and that is definiteness of purpose, the knowledge of what one wants, and the burning desire to possess it." In truth, having clarity of purpose is very important for every kind of aspiration or ambition in life because if you don't have a clearly defined vision and purpose for the things you want, you will never know the right steps to take towards achieving them. Think about it, people who are constantly striving to achieve something meaningful in life crave for clarity of purpose because for them, it's like focusing a clear source of light on their goals and aspirations so that they can see them clearly and work towards their attainment.

Amazingly, God wired you in a way that is peculiar to your purpose. You have the features you have because of the peculiarity of your assignment on earth. There is an environment where you can thrive, and there are others where you will struggle and feel like a failure. The fish can only survive in the water because that is the way it is wired. When you put a fish on land, you have given it a death sentence. It cannot survive on land. Why? It is not wired for the land. Being in a place, you are not wired for will only leave you frustrated and unproductive. This is why you have to discover your area of uniqueness and be very sure about it. Each of us is born with a unique purpose in life; and discovering, acknowledging, and fulfilling this purpose is perhaps the most important action that you'll take in life.

It will be impossible for you to achieve a vision you are not structured for. As powerful as the lion is, you cannot expect him to aim for the skies. If he keeps aiming for a thousand years, the law of gravity will always pull him down. He won't reach the skies because his natural abilities and talents are a clear indication that he simply can't! So before you write down that vision, be sure that it is something you are made for. Putting all your energy into something you are not made for will sap out your energy and still leave you unfulfilled.

So ask yourself, "What am I made for?"

The answer to this question may not come as early as you want it to. Give yourself enough time to get all the certainty and assurance you need. Don't jump into anything because people think you'll do well with it. God is your maker; He is the One who can give you the most accurate description of your life. Seek His face. As you speak to Him; pay attention to the inner yearning of your heart, and also to the little details around you. Give place to the witness within you. Look within you and take note of those things that come to you naturally - those things that you love to do passionately. This is the right thing to do because you were born with an inner compass that shows you how to harness your inherent qualities and abilities, so that your vision may come to pass.

We often spend most of our lives without having a vision (direction) or purpose in life. We follow professional and social scripts that are given by our fellow human beings instead of following our Creator's divine plan and intention for every one of us to live a fulfilled purposeful life. Unfortunately, by doing what others expect of us, or what the society we live in pushes us to do, we find ourselves feeling lost and uninspired by the small role we are playing in our lives and society. And in reality, feeling lost in life can be a sad experience that will rub you of happiness, a sense of fulfillment, and inner peace if left to linger for long.

However, the feeling of being lost without vision (direction) or purpose can be overcome with the right thought process and action steps if done from a godly perspective. But before I go any further, I want you to know that you are not the only one with this feeling of emptiness when it seems like you can't find your purpose in life. I remember vividly that during my final year at the university, I struggled within myself in existential bouts, trying to figure out exactly what my purpose on this earth was. And this lingered for a long time until I decided to surrender all to God and live according to His plans and intention for me.

I eventually uncovered my purpose and found my calling, but this was after years of really digging deep within me, as well as reading a lot of scriptures on the subject. Now that I have found my purpose and all is working out well for me, I feel like the most ideal and valuable thing to do is share what I know with you. So, based on my own experience and other materials that I was exposed to over the years, this book was carefully and thoughtfully put together to walk you through the steps that I used to find out who I am and what exactly God placed me on this earth to do.

Frankly speaking, finding your purpose in life can really be complicated and frustrating if you don't know how to dig deep to uncover certain simple truths about yourself. But the good news is that you don't have to do this alone; if you allow me to hold your hands, I will show you how to uncover and fulfill your purpose in life through the steps I have provided here. And when you eventually get clarity on what to do, when you know exactly what you exist for, who you truly are, and what your outlook in life should be, don't just stop there.

When you discover purpose, that purpose becomes your vision. It becomes the future you see; it becomes the dream in your heart. It becomes the reason why you are living. Your vision becomes your life guide; the explanation for the things you do and those you don't. The future you see becomes so strong and unbending to the things happening around you. The picture you have and see in your mind can never be erased by the pictures you see in circumstances.

If everybody else consumes everything they lay their hands on, the athlete knows he can't. Instead of wasting time in a music school, an athlete would rather spend his time training on the field. He has a vision; he has a picture in his heart, and he has been able to identify those things that will help him achieve it and those that won't. Even if everyone he knows chooses a path, he doesn't join the crowd because he knows exactly where he is headed due to his clarity of purpose.

You need to understand your vision, its peculiarities, and its demands. Achieving anything in life demands intentionality; being deliberate about every decision you make and every step you take. A vision-driven individual is not here today and there tomorrow; his vision keeps him on track. He is clear about what he wants and where he is headed. As you write down your vision, highlight your uniqueness; learn from others but don't try to be like them. Appreciate your individuality; create an image of your future by engaging the power of imagination. Highlight the demands of your vision. What sacrifices will you have to pay? What will you need to do? In any case, always remember that it's very important to discover and understand your vision because it represents your best knowledge of God's plan and purpose for your life.

RATIONALISE YOUR VISION

You must sit down with the vision you have discovered and rationalize the height. God will give you the picture of what He wired you to fulfill, that is your purpose on earth, but the scope which will represent the height and extent you will go will be defined by you. This is where planning comes in as you step out of your comfort zone into your purpose. To see destiny fulfilled in a grand style, planning is non-negotiable.

When you fail to plan, you are planning to fail. Success is not an accident, and it is not achieved by luck or chance; you have to position yourself in a way that you can attract success through a combination of planned and well-thought-out actions that you take at targeted intervals. Preparation positions you for success. Preparing for your vision requires that you spell out everything you'll need on the journey and how to get them. When you fail to prepare, you give room for anything to happen, positive or negative. The automaker, Henry Ford said, *"Before everything else, getting ready is the secret of success."*

God understands the importance of preparation, and that was why He said to Habakkuk in Habakkuk 2:2 (NKJV): *"Write the vision; make it plain on tablets, so he may run who reads it."* You must put your vision down in writing so you can be constantly reminded to run with it. Put it down on paper so it can show you the way to go. Any vision not documented is a vision that will not be pursued.

Who goes on a journey without counting the cost? Who sets out on a trip he is not prepared for? Ask yourself what you need to do before your vision can be actualized; this is how to prepare. Understanding your vision is being able to identify what you want; preparation is recognizing how to get it. When organizations are set up, they have a vision and mission statement; the vision is their target, it states where they are headed, while the mission states how the vision will be achieved, it tells what will be done in order to achieve the vision. What is your life mission? How do you intend to achieve your vision?

Nothing beats failure more than preparedness. Nothing beats failure more than preparedness. This statement seems simple, but when you dig a little deeper and probe a bit further, it reveals that a lot more can be achieved when a task is executed after proper prior preparation. According to the Merriam – Webster dictionary, 'preparation' is defined as "the action or process of making something ready for use or service or of getting ready for some occasion, test, or duty." So, preparation is definitely required to succeed in any chosen endeavor of life. I mean, you can't have a vision for something and then expect it to just happen without preparing well enough for its excellent execution.

Interestingly, discovering your vision and planning towards fulfilling it is like the work process of a master sculptor who slowly and carefully chips away from the stone in order to reveal the masterpiece of his handiwork eventually. What this is trying to imply is that not only do you need to understand and cultivate your vision, you also need to apply planning and creativity for the practical as well as a purposeful application of your vision. So learn a new skill if you have to, break away from some friends if you must, delay gratification, and then surround yourself with people who will propel you towards the fulfillment of your purpose. Don't live your life by chance. Don't live expecting that an opportunity will come your way. Opportunity always meets with preparation. Do all that you need to do before expecting a miracle to happen. God only blesses what we do. When we do nothing, we leave him with nothing to bless.

Mercy was just one of the girls who lived on the street; she was one of those girls with a humble home. But it was evident that Mercy was born to be a singer. You would hear her voice almost every morning running scales and exercising her voice. This young lady was in virtually every Christian music group in the neighborhood. If Mercy went to a birthday party or any sort of gathering at all, she would beg to be allowed to deliver a piece. She had no money to record her songs properly in a studio, but she kept doing all she could to prepare herself for the studio.

One day, one of the influential men in the area thought of giving back to society. He organized a talent hunt for youths and teenagers in the area. Mercy was at the contest, and she emerged as a winner. Some may be quick to say she was just lucky. *Lucky* is a terrible way of underrating the hard work attached to success. Luck undermines the value of hard work. Mercy wasn't lucky; she was prepared for success. This is what happens when you are prepared; it looks as if luck shined on you, but in the real sense, you already put in the required effort. If you cross your legs waiting for some miracle, nothing in your life will change.

Before launching out fully in pursuit and fulfillment of your vision, create a vision board that will help you come up with strategies as well as work out the modalities on how to bring your vision to life. Additionally, place yourself on the path to the actualization of your vision through visualization and meditation, which are essential mind exercises and preparation required before you can take meaningful actions.

In fact, whenever you visualize or mediate prayerfully intending to bring your vision to life, you are emitting positive energy and a powerful frequency which aligns with God and his purpose for your life. Start investing in your future; start sowing seeds. God's blessing is the rain that falls on the seed planted. When we plant nothing, the rain falls on bare ground and does nothing to it. Pray and commit your ways to God. Unless the Lord builds a house, the builders labor in vain (Psalm 127:1). Proverbs 16:3 (NAS) says, *"Commit your works to the Lord, and your plans will be established."*

Though things may not go as planned, prepare all the same. Keep shaping your future by confessing God's Word. The power of life and death both lie in the tongue. Take charge of the future. Life is full of surprises, but when you are prepared for life, you know how to handle those surprises. One of Warren Buffett's quotes states that *"an idiot with a plan can beat a genius without a plan"*.

PURSUE YOUR VISION

This is what it actually means to step into your vision. This is where you start doing the very thing you were called to be. After Paul hid away for some years in preparation for ministry work, he came out and started what he was called to do. His passion and commitment to the work were even more than that of some of the apostles who had been with Jesus.

By the time Apostle Paul started his ministry, he knew the exact thing to do; he knew the people he was called to witness to. He was not headed in different directions. His focus was single. In the place of preparation, he had received direction that he was called to the Gentiles, and those were the people he approached with his gospel.

Like Paul, we must focus mainly on a single vision. We cannot be pursuing many things at the same time and expect results. Divided focus yields no result; in the end, you fail here, and you fail there. Hence the saying: "Jack of all trades, master of none." When you focus on one thing, you are able to put all of your energy into that one thing in order to boost your attentiveness and productivity towards seeing that one thing through. For instance, if you have been called to be a pastor, focus on finding out where you should be and the people you have been called to preach to.

Take action. Don't just go about compiling many lists of different things to do and how to do them; take action and start doing what you can do with those things that are already available to you. Nike says in her advert, "Just do it". Push yourself; give yourself all the motivation you need to work. Find people around you can tap strength from. Place yourself in the company of people who inspire you to be more, people who can teach and motivate you to take action. Place yourself around people of like minds who can challenge you to do and be more with your life.

Many people spend years doing nothing under the guise that they are making preparations. Eventually, there'd be no difference between them and those who never discovered purpose. It is time to start doing something. A perfect time may never come; you may not have all the needed resources now, but just go ahead. Everything will fall in place as you carry out the idea. When you lack motivation, think about the people whose blessings are attached to your seriousness. That perfect time you are waiting for may never come. You will have to create the perfect time yourself. You won't have everything in place; start anyway.

You don't have to wait to be perfect before stepping into your vision. It doesn't have to be all figured out. The basic thing required is knowledge about the field you're delving into and openness to learning. As you function in your vision, you become more empowered to fulfill it. Until you step into you, you may not know what is inside of you. Until I answered the call of God to go into ministry, I never imagined myself being a people's person. Those hidden treasures will never surface until you really do it.

Focusing on the excuses and the many things that are not available will give you more reasons never to try. As a matter of fact, if you continue to make excuses to the extent that they begin to pile up, you will eventually become complacent. Unfortunately, complacency doesn't lead to growth; it only leads to stagnation and going back to old habits. So, once the most important things are set, just start! Talk to people; ask them for help, and counsel. Proverbs 15:22 makes it clear that *"Without consultation, plans are frustrated; but with many counselors, they succeed."*

Just start; I know it sounds too simple, but everything else you need will surely fall into place as you carry on. Avoid procrastination because it will only compound the problems or challenges that you will face along the way. However, as you go ahead with the pursuit of your vision, you will gain more clarity. Even though challenges may spring up, you will know how to tackle them one after the other. So, quit bringing up the excuse, "I don't know how to go about it." When you start, you will know how to go about it.

PAY THE PRICE

My reverend, mentor, and father; Dr. David O. Oyedepo, made a profound statement "Nothing of value is free". If your future is great, then you will be expected to invest greatly in it. Be ready to pay the price for greatness if greatness is your choice.

No one said it would be an easy journey; you'll have to pay the price. There is no way that we can avoid the fact that achieving any type of success or meaningful venture demands something of real value from us. We can't achieve anything that means something to us by just wishing for it or wanting it; there is a price that must be paid. In fact, the higher your vision, the bigger the price you have to pay. So when the going seems tough, and everything appears to be falling apart, you have to stand strong and keep up with the race knowing that you must pay the price to achieve the desired outcome. Jesus Christ had many reasons to pull out and say He would not go ahead and redeem man, but He understood the magnitude of the responsibility upon Him. He chose to endure all the pain because of the glory He saw ahead of Him. He knew that if He failed to pay the price, He would also miss the glory waiting for Him. That was one motivation for Him.

There will be times when everything will become bleak; things may just start failing, important people may begin to pull out of the vision, anything could be the case, but still, you'd have to keep your head high. Think of the glory ahead of you. Find something to motivate you on your weak days to keep on pushing and never lose sight of your vision until you get to that space and place that you were destined for. Don't give room for slackness or give up, no matter how difficult the journey might seem.

Running with your vision would require some denials. Certain things will entice you, but you'd have to look away from them because the vision will be at stake. Pay the price. In the end, it will be worth it. In the same vein, you will be required to do certain things that you wouldn't do ordinarily. Do these things. Let the future you see be a driving force. The picture of the future will provoke and release some inner force that will propel you to keep moving until there is fulfillment. Zeal and perseverance are required to drive you and keep you on track; naturally, you will pursue what you see already without allowing surrounding circumstances to deter you.

As much as the Holy Spirit wants to help you, He needs you to be willing to receive the help. Only cowards back out at the show of the slightest challenge. Vision-oriented people keep running the race, tackling every obstacle until the end of the race. Give yourself to learning in that area; read about those who have walked in that path before. Learn lessons from them so you can find the journey easier.

Gold must pass through the fire to become a bar of refined gold. Coal goes under intense pressure to produce diamonds; the iron needs to pass through the fire to be shaped and become a prized possession. There is no position without opposition. Yes; your Canaan has giants you must overcome to occupy it. You must choose to rise above all challenges in life, knowing that the sacrifices you make and endure today, lays the foundation for the victories you will celebrate and enjoy tomorrow. So, for whatever reason, don't give up. Yes! Every new level will attract new devils, but you have the unction to function and fulfill the mandate on your life, don't cave in, don't give in, don't give up, keep going; The One who has called you is faithful; He will remain committed to you through it all. Keep saying to yourself: *I can do all things through Christ who strengthens me.*

REMAIN CONSISTENT

Consistency is the sustainer of any business and any destiny. It is what marks the difference between a successful and an unsuccessful person. Consistency is what keeps you going till the end of the line, until the point when the vision is finally accomplished. No matter how well prepared you are, everything will fail in the absence of consistency. When the passion and motivation are high, it is very easy to set out and start pursuing your vision, but as time passes and the passion begins to wane, there is a tendency to lose interest and stop doing the things you used to do. However, when we understand why consistency is an important habit to have, we can use it to our advantage in staying committed and dedicated to carrying out all the necessary tasks needed to bring our vision to fruition.

Ask sportspersons; there is power in doing a particular thing over and over again. If you want to get the desired result, you must remain consistent with what you do. Leadership guru John Maxwell said, "Small disciplines repeated with consistency every day lead to great achievements gained slowly over time." The vision doesn't just materialize supernaturally; it is the consistency that brings your vision to the point of actualization. Brian Tracy also said, "The person we believe ourselves to be will always act in a manner consistent with our self-image." We have to place the picture of who we want to be and consistently act like it before we can actually see it materialize.

You have to keep the passion alive always. You have to cultivate the habit of doing the same thing repeatedly until we get what we want. There isn't really anything we can achieve without being consistent. Even our walk with God is based on consistency. Suppose you lack consistency in your relationship with God. In that case, your intimacy with Him will suffer because consistency is the key to developing a close relationship in our spiritual walk with Him. We cannot be on with God and off tomorrow and still expect to have a flaming relationship with Him. We have to remain patient and consistent until the work of salvation is completed in us.

"Anyone who begins to plow a field but keeps looking back is of no use in the kingdom of God." – Luke 9:62 (NCV)

Honestly speaking, God hates inconsistency because nothing seems to turn people away from Christianity today more than inconsistency. Webster's Ninth New Collegiate Dictionary defines 'Inconsistency' as – "not being persistent, lacking firmness of constitution (conviction) or character, and lacking harmony of conduct or practice with a profession." If you review and observe once again the last sentence on the definition of 'inconsistency' – "lacking harmony of conduct or practice with a profession," you will see that it is a statement of fact which reminds us of a very popular adage which says: "Practice what you preach." So, as you can see, inconsistency is very detrimental to our walk with God as Christians. Once you begin the journey, you must demonstrate a high level of consistency in order to stay focused till the job is done. Inconsistency makes you unfit for the kingdom. When you start, don't stop because you lost interest, and then start again when the interest is restored. You must be true to the course. It is the Father's assignment; it must not be handled with levity. No matter how urgent the situation is, your consistent time and walk with God must be an integral part of your life. Keep your eyes on the plough and never look back.

James 1:4 says, *"Let perseverance finish its work so that you may be mature and complete, not lacking anything."*

God places a demand on us to remain consistent, and enduring every phase of our journey till we come into full maturity in Him. If you give up along the line, you will also be giving up the vision and the sense of fulfillment that comes with it. Your vision lies in hope, waiting to be brought alive. Fulfilling God's vision for your life is a very demanding and difficult venture; so there will be times when you will find yourself flirting with the idea of giving up. However, you can't afford to give up; let it not be an option that crosses your heart. As you set out, do so with the mindset to not back out until the vision is accomplished.

Until the journey comes to an end, it is not over. Your fulfillment of purpose here on earth is still in place until you die. So, you can't quit until it's finally over. There will be hurdles along the way; there will be reasons not to go on, but you must decide to remain consistent until you have fulfilled the Father's mind.

Like Jesus Christ, let your confession be: "My nourishment comes from doing the will of God, who sent me, and from finishing his work. Jesus said to them, 'My food is to do the will of Him who sent me and to accomplish it." The calling must be accomplished, and the assignment must be completed. There is no reward for those who start and don't end; the reward is reserved for those who remain faithful to the end.

James 1:12 says, *"Blessed is the one who **perseveres** under trial because, having stood the test, that person will receive the crown of life that the Lord has promised to those who loves Him."*

You have to persevere because it won't be easy getting there. In fact, perseverance and persistence are equally crucial and important in the work required to bring your vision to a place of fruition, given the challenges and obstacles that you are most likely to face along the way. Without any hint of doubt, you will surely have reasons to give up, but you must stand the test of time so that you can receive the crown of life promised to us.

Step in but don't find a reason to step out. Find a reason to remain until you make an impact. Now that you are in do not stop or look back, you have no business with where you are coming from. Look forward to the prize ahead. You will surely make it without a doubt.

CHAPTER THREE

STEP UP

Now that you have stepped into your vision and purpose, it's time to step up. Until you step up the vision, you might never make a difference. You must create a unique trademark that singles you out of the crowd. You cannot make a difference if you are afraid to be different. You must step up to be different, knowing that distinction is an integral part of God's creation. He designed and created you to be a unique brand.

You know what a piece of freshly baked cake from the oven looks like; bare, plain, and without color. If it is placed on display, no one goes close to it because it attracts no one. It may be very delicious, but nobody is drawn to it because it lacks beauty. On the other hand, imagine a well-decorated cake set on display; people would naturally be drawn to it because of its beauty and attractiveness. While the undecorated cake remains untouched, the decorated one would have been bought.

This is the case for many of us. We are like that plain cake, bare and unattractive. We claim to be fulfilling a purpose;

doing what we've been called to do, but we're undecorated and lack an appealing identity. We're too ordinary to attract anyone's attention and admiration. We are too unattractive to even reach those we've been sent to. It is not enough to do what we should do; we must do it with a touch of creativity and excellence. We must do it in such a way that people want to come and be blessed through us. The creativity we add to our work is the icing on the cake; it is the reason people would love to have a taste of us.

There is a wide gap between a job that is done for the sake and that done to make a difference. The former is what most of us do; we walk in purpose because we know the danger that comes with not walking in it; not necessarily because we want to make a change in our world and bring glory to God. As you step into your vision, you need to step up your imagination and creativity. Contrary to popular belief, we all possess the ability to create something of real value that makes a whole lot of difference if we really put our minds to it. God gave you the mandate to be a co-creator when He created you in the first place, so if you want your works to go far enough to draw many people's attention, you need to be creative and do your things with a touch of imagination and excellence. This is highly important because creativity and excellence are a central source of meaning in our lives since our Creator is an excellent God.

"Whatever your hand finds to do, do it with your might, for there is no work or thought or knowledge or wisdom in Sheol, to which you are going." – Ecclesiastes 9:10-11 (NRS)

Whatever has been committed into your hands must be done with all diligence. Strive to be the best at whatever you are doing. David was so skillful and anointed in playing the harp that as an ordinary boy, he was called on to come and minister to the king whenever he was in distress. His excellence, and his ability to play the harp the way no one else would, earned him the privilege. God has called a lot of pastors, but the only thing that will make you stand out is your individuality and uniqueness. This is why Solomon said in Proverbs 22:29 (NAS): *"Do you see a man skillful in his work? He will stand before kings; he will not stand before obscure men."* In the message translation, it says, *"Observe people who are good at their work— skilled workers are always in demand and admired; they don't take a backseat to anyone."*

Don't settle for mediocrity; don't just carry on for the sake of it. Carry on because the vision must be accomplished. Spice up your work; hone your skills and don't be lackadaisical. Be daring, bold, and brave so that you can accomplish bigger and better things in life. In short, you must always be willing to step up by giving your 100% and nothing less.

"How many are your works, Lord! Lord! In wisdom, you made them all; the earth is full of creatures. There is a sea, vast and spacious, teeming with creatures without number – living things both large and small." – Psalm 104:24-25

Our God Himself is creative, and we are made in His image. We also have His creative ability; we can make things up with our thoughts and words. We can create and recreate. We can imagine and bring to life. A look at the skies and the trees and all the works of nature makes it clear that God is creative. He could have made just one species of fish; all the earth could have been painted green – the sky, the land, the plants, the waters; there could have been just one kind of everything, but now, God is creative. He is imaginative and innovative. He thinks something in His heart and brings it into reality by His words.

"Then God said, 'Let us make mankind in our image, in our likeness, so that they may rule over the fish in the sea and the birds in the sky, over the livestock and all the wild animals, and overall the creatures that move along the ground. So God created mankind in His own image, in the image of God He created them; male and female He created them." – Genesis 1:26-27

God first conceived the thought in His heart; He carefully ruminated upon it before creating you and me. The creation of man was premeditated. When it was time, God gave life to His thoughts by making man. We are like God, too; we have a mind to imagine and hands to create. In other words, we are created to reflect the image and likeness of our Creator. He is the most magnificent creative being ever to exist, we as His creations and co-creators are expected to reflect the same qualities. To achieve this, you must be willing and ready to use the natural gifts that God has given you to honor him and live a purposeful life of vision with passion, faithfulness, and a commitment to excellence. So as you do your work, don't be satisfied with the little achievements here and there. Look for areas where you can achieve better and greater things. Step up your game.

No two miracles were done in the same way. God chose to display His power in different unpredictable ways. This is why there are many dimensions to knowing Him. God is not restricted to one pattern. He will do ten things in ten different ways. We also have this mental ability. We can expand the capacity of our mind to think beyond its borders. We can think of new ways to tackle our challenges. We can do without running out of ideas, and to do this, we have to key into our God-given power and ability to create.

God gave man something powerful that made him superior to all the other animals; God gave us His nature, and the ability to think and process our thoughts. Animals don't have this; this is why scientists call them lower animals. This is why, like God, we can invent things. Our minds can paint a picture, and our hands can give life to that picture. As God's children, our imagination has been infused into divinity, and there's no limit to what we can create. Like our Father, we are creative beings without limitations. In fact, God has given us two roles regarding creation: exercising both dominion and stewardship over the earth. Our understanding of dominion is that it is unlimited, and it is intended to ensure that our creativity flows and functions properly, thereby accomplishing God's plan and purposes. Stewardship on the other hand is particularly connected with caring appropriately for God's creation.

So, as it is there's no limit to the imaginative power of the mind. As long as we are ready to use it, there is no end to what we can imagine and create. Except we choose to be lazy in thinking, we can be the very best at what we do. The only limit we can face is the wall we build around our minds, which causes our inability to think deeply and creatively. You cannot be shallow in thinking and expect great things to come from you because great things are birthed from the place of reflection. It is by exercising your mind that new ideas and inventions reveal themselves to you. To put it in simple terms, you can become or achieve anything that your mind is mentally able to visualize and imagine.

The mind is the factory of explosive manifestation. Everything that we do begins from the mind. If it is not thought about in the mind, it cannot be carried out. What this means is that the power of the mind has the ability to make or break your success in life – therefore, you should strive to become the master of your own mind. This is why Jesus said to the disciples in Matthew 15:18: *"For the things that come out of a person's mouth come from the heart; and they defile the man."* The mind is the seat of our thoughts and imagination. We can wield it in the right direction to get the desired result. Joel Annesley, a life coach, and author, said: "Your mind is precious. It has the power to help you unlock infinite possibilities."

The quality of your life is based on the quality of your mind. How you think is how you live. Proverbs 23:7 (NKJV) says, *"For as he thinks in his heart, so is he..."* If you want to change the quality of your life, you have to change the way you think. If you want to upgrade your vision, you will need to upgrade your mind. You cannot expect to keep thinking the same way and see results different from what you've always seen.

God understands the power of the mind. He knows that whatever is conceived in the mind will always find expression. This was why He stopped the people of the earth before they went far with building the tower that would reach the heavens. He knew they could achieve it if they set their hearts to it.

"Then they said, 'Come, let us build ourselves a city with a tower that reaches the heavens so that we may make a name for ourselves; otherwise we will be scattered over the face of the whole earth."(Genesis 11:4).

Before they started carrying out their plan, it was just a thought in their hearts. But as they thought about it, and discussed it, it started to come alive. This was why God scattered their language, so the mission would not be accomplished. If God saw the possibility of that seemingly impossible task simply because they nursed the thought, how much more our little dreams and aspirations that will not even take centuries to materialize? The mind is powerful; only those who understand its power can fully maximize it. There are no borders around the mind; it is unlimited, so are the things that can come from it. Dare to imagine. Dare to dream.

In the course of pursuing your vision, don't let challenges or loss of interest be the reason you back out. If challenges persist, you must be able to think of new ways to solve the problems. You will always find life in whatever you do if you don't keep doing it the same way; you have to diversify and create different ways to do the same thing. Don't be streamlined to a single pattern. Don't be afraid to explore. Try new things, and you will see new results.

Pray to God and ask Him to help you with your mind. In prayers, let your imagination be at work. Thinking and imagination are crucial when asking God. It shapes our prayer and informs our decision making and the next line of action and steps to be taken. When we pray with a blank mind, it appears as though we don't really know what we want, like as if we are just open to anything. This is a bad attitude and approach to life – to leave everything to chance. You must take charge of your life by controlling your mind and more specifically, your thoughts because both your mind and thoughts are the most powerful tools you have for the creation of your reality. The truth is that when you commit to taking charge of your life by developing your mindset and thought process, you'll have more control to start making positive changes that will eventually bring joy, happiness, and fulfillment into your life.

Ephesians 3:20 (NKJV) says, *"Now to Him who is able to do exceedingly abundantly above all that we can ask or think, according to His power that works in us."*

God's ears are open to not just our prayers, but also the imaginations of our heart. He grants the requests of our mouths and hearts way beyond what we expect. We cannot afford to allow anything to grow around our minds. This is why Paul said in Philippians 4:8: *"Finally, brothers and sisters, whatever is true, whatever is noble, whatever is right, whatever is pure, whatever is lovely, whatever is admirable – if anything is excellent or praiseworthy- think about such things."* Be sure that your thoughts are right, and in accordance with God's Word because you will not only have more than you ask, you will also have more than you imagine.

If you've been doing the same thing the same way for years, it is time to step up. It is time to become an authority at what you do. If you remain at the level of an ordinary amateur, you won't ever get there. Look for paths where no one has ever walked and be fearless enough to go in there. Bring up things no one has ever done. To find and own your own unique space, you must be ready to travel on a lonely road that is less travelled. I'm sure this is why the Bible in Mathew 7:13-14 says, *"Because narrow is the gate and difficult is the way which leads to life, there are a few who find it."*

If you are supposed to be a preacher, relax and have reflective moments on how to go about it. Yes, every preacher has a congregation, every preacher preaches, every church has a choir but sit down and ask yourself this question, "What can I do differently? What has anyone never tried?" When you find out, implement it in your church and watch the difference, it will make. A singer must find himself, and what makes him different from 1000 other singers he must discover his individuality and develop it. Until he does so, he may not be able to step up in the pursuit of his vision.

We must understand that God has blessed us to be a blessing. Our gifts and calling are not really about us. They are more about the people we are sent to bless. We must be sure that what we are doing is enough to draw them in and get them blessed. If they cannot relate to what we do, then it is almost impossible for them to be blessed by what we do. For the sake of these people, spend time reflecting on better ways to do your thing.

To be that person you were born to be, you must cultivate the spirit of innovation; the ability to bring something out of nothing. Don't be satisfied with mediocrity. With God, you can't sit on the fence. You have to be either here or there. You have to be doing it well or not doing it at all. Maximize the creative power of your mind to unleash all the untapped things around you. There are untapped resources lying fallow, resources that will waste away if you fail to use your mind creatively. It is only when you use your mind that your eyes will be open to the many opportunities around you.

Your service is to God; He is the One who will reward you in heaven and on earth. In whatever you do, carry the consciousness that you are accountable to God. Even If you do any other thing, don't handle your calling with levity. It is the yardstick with which you will be rewarded. Use your gifts for the expansion of the kingdom. Colossians 3:23-24 (WEB) says, *"Whatever you do, work heartily, as for the Lord and not men, knowing that from the Lord you will receive the reward of inheritance; for you serve the Lord Christ."*

This is the Father's business. You must be determined to do it with all your might. Use your mind, your words, and actions to uncover and fulfill your God-given vision. In short, if only you can imagine the greatness of God, the One who created the world, you would never settle for less. You are a child of the living God – created in His image and likeness; so know your worth, and step up!

CHAPTER FOUR

STEP ON

It is very normal to encounter obstacles on the road to destiny. As a matter of fact, they are always positioned at strategic points as you go. The path to destiny is often speckled with hurdles, disappointments, unexpected circumstances, and struggles. The purpose of these hurdles is to frustrate you, make you lose hope, and let go of the vision. But you know, challenges do not have the power to consume your dreams unless you let them. In fact, when you encounter challenges or hit hurdles in life, don't let them be a hindrance to your goals and aspirations; jump them, go around them, through them or under them, but no matter what, never let them stop you from moving forward.

As you draw close to the fulfillment of your purpose, you need to step on all the obstacles and challenges that spring up. You must not allow yourself to be consumed. There will be limitations from within and around. You may not find help in places where you expect them to come from on a normal basis. Friends and family may not totally support, and worst of all, your plan may seem not to be coming through. Despite all this, you must keep the vision alive, knowing that you have God on your side to see you through. As long as God is in the boat with you, you will get to the other side.

The challenges that show up on the journey towards destiny come in different forms. Some challenges spring up from your personal life, such as the state of your mind and psychological well-being; there are also challenges influenced by people around you and those caused by unforeseen circumstances. At different points, you will be faced with one or more challenges of these kinds. You need to garner enough strength ahead of time so that you can withstand the tough times. If you fall on the day of adversity, then your inner strength and desire to become the best version of yourself is weak. This is not in any way trying to make lite of the fact that moving forward and never giving up during tough times of hardship is extremely difficult and challenging, but one thing that is certain as well as the fact that change is constant; so whatever bumps and obstacles that emerge on your way today will eventually fizzle out provided you keep pushing for a change in such an unwanted situation. Moreover, the willingness and resilience to continuously keep moving forward in the face of adversity is an attitude that will ensure your breakthrough in many areas and aspects of life.

"Adversity causes some men to break, and some others to break records." –William Arthur Ward.

A goal-getter never gives up until his goal has been achieved. He keeps pushing through until he reaches the finishing line. You must possess the power to endure, and the ability to face defeat repeatedly without giving up. You must find a reason to hang on till it's finally over. You must have heard the saying, "It is not over until it is over". It means you cannot quit until it is time to quit. Refuse to be drowned in troubles, however daunting and challenging they might appear to be. As a matter of fact, you must be ready to confront your struggles, knowing that "Tough times never last, but tough people do," as was said by Robert Schuller. No matter what the challenge is, you should approach it with the belief that "this too shall pass."

Holding on despite the troubles that come your way is a manifestation that you have strong convictions about your future. You should not see the actualization of your vision as optional; instead, see it as a necessity. Giving up at the show of the slightest challenge is a sign that you do not really have firm convictions about where you're headed. Tough and challenging times are inevitable, but when you face challenges in life with the belief that God has already given you the power to overcome hardships, you will go on to break difficult barriers and experience fulfillment by doing so.

God, Himself has left us a good example. He has shown that He doesn't give up. In His plan to redeem man, He patiently waited through centuries and generations until the perfect time came. He didn't give up on man; He wasn't frustrated by man's sin and disregard for Him. Instead, He waited patiently until the appointed time. We should learn this from our Father. God doesn't give up; we also must not give up until the vision is fully accomplished.

Joseph believed in his dreams; he believed that one day, his brothers would bow down for him. Though things did not turn out as imagined, he did not give up on his dreams. Who could have even thought that the hurdles were actually taking him to the place of destiny? He could have become reckless in a foreign land, he could have let go of his integrity, but he didn't. He held his identity firmly in God until his dreams came alive.

KNOW THAT GOD IS WITH YOU

The reason why many of us quickly back out and give up on our calling is that we think we are all by ourselves. But this is not true; God is always with us. We may not see Him or feel Him, but He's always there. The words of Jesus to us as He left the earth were: *"I will be with you always, even to the end of age."* If He made that commitment to us, then He is always with us.

Lean on God's strength and wisdom to deal with your hurdles because your own strength will fail you. Isaiah 12:2 says, *"Surely God is my salvation; I will trust and not be afraid. The Lord, the Lord Himself is my strength and my defense; He has become my salvation."* God is there every step of the way to save you from your struggles. You must lean on God's power to save and keep you until victory is finally won.

"For the eyes of the Lord are over the righteous, and His ears are open to their prayer. But the face of the Lord is against those who do evil." (1 Peter 3:12 NKJV). God's eyes are over us, and His ears are open to our prayers. He is ever attentive.

You don't have to complain in frustration when you are confused about how to proceed and move forward in life. The Holy Spirit has been given to guide us and show us the way. When you are confused about where to turn, seek counsel from Him, and He will make way for you.

Jude 1:24 says, *"To Him who is able to keep you from stumbling and to present you before His glorious presence without fault and with great joy."* He will hold us up and keep us from falling away. The masters of this world give assignments to their servants and leave them to themselves to get the work done, but God is not like them. He has taken us in as His children and has put it upon Himself to help us walk through this journey.

> *"So do not fear, for **I am with you**. Don't be discouraged, for I am God. I will strengthen you and help you. I will hold you up with my victorious hands."* (Isaiah 41:10 NLT)

There is an assurance from God's word in Jeremiah 1:19 (KJ), *"And they shall fight against thee; but they shall not prevail against thee; for I am with thee, saith the LORD, to deliver thee."* You have no reason to fret in the middle of a crisis; God is with

64

you there, talk to Him. Even though your friends may disappoint you and things may not just add up, be confident in God. You have to rest assured that there is a God who will never leave your side even if everyone else does.

BE EXPECTANT OF MIRACLES

As you cross the hurdles and fight the challenges, never lose hope. Jesus has informed us beforehand that we will be faced with trials on the journey of faith, but we must take heart because He has overcome. The night cannot last forever; the morning will surely come. Trust God to show up for you in miraculous ways. Don't fight with pessimism like people who do not know the Lord. You have a superior power at work in you. As you pray to God, be expectant of miracles and wonders.

See your challenges as an opportunity for God to reveal Himself, not a chance for you to be swallowed up. Face your battles with the assurance that you are a winner. Job said in Job 42:2 (NKJV), *"I know that **you can do everything** and that no purpose of yours can be withheld from you."* If God caused the day to stand still for the sake of His children, if He parted the seas for His people, if He raised Jesus from the dead, what will He not do for us? He cannot be restrained by anything; all power and dominion are in His hands. We have seen how God, on many occasions, showed up to deliver His people and save them from distress. No challenge is greater than God's power; even the laws of nature obey Him so, He can channel everything for your good.

Joshua recognized the presence of God with them as the Israelites fought against the Canaanites. If they did not win that battle, they would not get to the Promised Land. He lifted His voice to God and made an unbelievable request: *"At that time, Joshua spoke to the Lord in the day when the Lord gave the Amorites over to the sons of Israel, and He said in the sight of Israel, 'Sun, stand still at Gibeon, and moon, in the valley of Aijalon. And the sun stood still, and the moon stopped until the nation took vengeance on their enemies. Is this not written in the book of Jashar? The sun stopped in the midst of heaven and did not hurry to set for about a whole day. There has been no day like it before or since, when the Lord heeded the voice of a man, for the Lord fought for Israel."* (Joshua 10:12-14).

What happened that day had never happened before in history, but God granted His request because He trusted God to show up for Him. God can also show up for you in miraculous ways – ways that no one has seen before. Focus on the magnitude of God's power, not the size of your problems. Let the words in Isaiah 43:1-3 strengthen you as they strengthen me: "Do not fear for I have redeemed you; I have summoned you by name; you are mine. When you pass through the waters, I will be with you; and when you pass through the rivers, they will not sweep you. When you walk through the fire, you will not be burned; the flames will not set you ablaze."

You should rejoice because the Lord is on your side. You will scale through every hurdle and challenge in this race because you are working under an insurmountable power. Don't let the obstacles be the reason you lose sight of your vision. If you stumble, God's hands are by your side to hold you up. In the end, everything will fall in place, and the vision will be accomplished. Instead of confessing misfortune, fear or lack, confess the assuring Word of God.

LEARN FROM YOUR CHALLENGES

Everything that happens to you is for a reason. As God's child, He will not permit the enemy to tamper with you. Romans 8:28 (NKJV) says, *"And we know that all things work together for the good of those who love God."* Our challenges, testimonies, failures, and successes work in unison for our good. So we must not despise our challenges. Instead, we must see them as stepping stones into a new phase of life; we must see them as a platform to become a better version of ourselves. As a matter of fact, you couldn't possibly have become the person you are today if you had not had to contend with adversity in the journey of your life thus far.

Mo Seetubtim wrote, "Sometimes, the uncomfortable things in life are there to teach us lessons because to go through a change of habit, we need to feel uncomfortable."

Challenges should push us to grow and help us become better versions of ourselves. As a child my Father made me understand that we human beings cannot avoid challenges because life is about ups and downs, and that instead of running away from my challenges, I should not only learn from them but also go ahead and face all my challenges wholeheartedly knowing that this is how I'll eventually become a stronger and better person in life. So whenever trouble springs up, keep your head up and remember some popular proverbial phrases or quotes that inspire positivity in the face of adversity like, "when life throws you lemons, make lemonade." So, what does this mean? With lemons representing sourness or bitterness in life, and lemonades meaning a desirable outcome, this means that you should always try to apply a positive attitude to a problem in such a way that ensures that you never back down or give up until the problem is either resolved to a satisfactory level, or used as a springboard to push yourself further, or even a combination of both. In any case, you must possess the persistency, tenacity, determination, and analytical ability to learn from any problematic or challenging situation. In this light, challenges can be seen as valid sources of inspiration and introspection that offers powerful and valuable life lessons for your personal growth and development. This is so because when challenges or problems arise, we receive a wake-up call and an urgent need for self-evaluation to understand the crux of the issues arising and addressing them immediately for our own good. So whenever you are confronted by trials and tribulations, rather than blame others for your challenges take responsibility and look inwards, just so that you can fully grasp and appreciate the possible life lessons to be learned from the challenges being experienced. Whether you are responsible directly or indirectly for the root cause of a problem or challenge, don't wallow in self-pity or dwell on the situation regretfully, instead try to initiate an inner conversation with yourself to know and acknowledge that which the challenge is exposing you to. This profound attitude and approach will not only help you identify the themes and things that usually cause challenges for you, but will also help you in facing your present predicament and other similar future challenges with clarity and courage.

There are some cases where the situation is totally beyond your control. For instance, you may lose a loved one or be involved in an accident. This will affect you greatly, but I'm not here to tell you that you should let it control you. When a situation is beyond your control, you can't control it, but you can control your actions. You can control how you react to it. If you allow the condition to go on, you will be subject to its wiles; but if you focus on looking at the situation from a different but an enlightening perspective that enables you to behold the light at the end of the tunnel, you will certainly experience the sun that shines from the calmness that comes after every storm.

You become stronger as a result of your experience. Each challenge you face and overcome makes you a lot stronger than you were before. You become more resilient and confident as you pass through every stage. James 1:2, 3 and 12, says, *"Consider it pure joy, my brothers and sisters, whenever you face trials of many kinds of friends because you know the testing of your faith produces perseverance... Blessed is the one who perseveres under trial, because having stood the test, that person will receive the crown of life that the Lord has promised to those who love Him."*

The Apostle Paul also expressed a similar perspective on adversity: *"We glory in tribulations also: knowing that tribulation worketh patience: and patience, experience; and experience, hope: And hope maketh not ashamed: because the love of God is shed abroad in our hearts by the Holy Ghost which is given unto us. For when we were yet without strength, in due time, Christ died for the ungodly"* (Romans 5: 3-6).

Pick up the lessons peculiar to every obstacle, understand it, and know how it works so you can know how to tackle subsequent ones. Only a fool keeps making the same mistakes repeatedly; only a fool makes himself vulnerable to the same thing over and over again. So prepare ahead of time; know how to avoid imminent dangers, and how to learn from them just in case they catch up with you. You have the wisdom of God, so that should inspire and strengthen you to actively overcome any challenging situation whenever it occurs.

TRIED AS GOLD

"But He knows the way that I take; when He has tested me, I will come forth as gold." (Job 23:10)

All the challenges we face have a purpose in God's hands. They are to help us become who God wants us to be. Before we can enjoy the glory that awaits us, we need to endure the present challenges that come our way. True maturity cannot come without having passed through the test of fire. So instead of complaining about yourself and comparing yourself with others, you should be glad about what is happening to you — you have a chance to come out better.

Job was an ordinary man like us; when his faith was tested, he lost every single thing he had, yet he did not find a reason to curse God. In his suffering, Job reminded God, *"Your hands shaped me and made me, will you now turn and destroy me? Remember that you molded me like clay. Will you now turn me to durst again?* (Job 10:8-9). Instead of whining about his problems, he chose to believe that God is working out something better for Him. By the time he came out of his troubles, he had regained a double portion of all the wealth and property he lost. Truly, he came forth as gold.

The process gold passes through before it becomes good to the eyes is not a very palatable one. Gold from the earth is full of dross and impurities; no one sees it and loves it as it is. If it is put on display, no one will go close to it. This is the way we all are at the beginning; we are ordinary, undeveloped, unrefined. Like gold, we have to go through the fire so that the beauty in

71

us can come out for the world to see. Our trials and difficulties are the fire that we pass through. When we come out of them victorious, we are better than what or how we used to be.

"And if children, then heirs; heirs of God and joint-heirs with Christ; if so be that we suffer from Him, that we may also be glorified together for I reckon that the sufferings of this present time are not worthy to be compared to the glory which shall be revealed to us." (Romans 8:17-18, KJ). If the trials appear to be too difficult to endure, consider the glory that awaits you after all is done. Let that hope strengthen you and keep you strong for the hurdles ahead.

The good thing is that these difficult times don't last forever. They are for a particular period which is only a small matter compared to what we will enjoy after we have endured. Every one of us has our own set of challenges and learning to overcome them will help us remain focused and calm under pressure. So, never see the obstacles on your way as too big to handle. No test will come your way that is bigger than your strength. Step on every one of them with the power of God at work in you. You cannot be consumed. Hurdles are supposed to be crossed, so see every stumbling block as a stepping stone for you to step on and cross over to a better side; challenges are there for you to overcome, so you will surely overcome them; trials are meant to be passed, so you will surely pass them all – through Christ who strengthens you!

Till the vision is achieved, there is no backing down, no giving up; there is no retreat, no surrender.

CHAPTER FIVE

STEP HIGH

There is a tendency for us to feel relaxed and satisfied with little achievements that we forget the big picture and the bigger goals yet to be achieved. Never should you over-celebrate your current state when there are still more strides to take. Never allow the euphoria of a single victory to keep you from moving forward towards achieving many other victories ahead. In 2003, while at the University of Portsmouth, I joined a prayer group, praying for the nation, fellow students, and lecturers. We prayed, asking for the best of the land and the grace to complete our course. In the middle of prayers, I heard in my spirit, "Don't settle for less, don't accept the best when there is the best of the best, don't stop until you are outstanding the best of the best." Those words stirred up an unusual drive that has never left me. I have never read it, but I heard God say it to me. I shared with my friends, and from that moment, I knew there was something greater ahead of me. Friends, I tell you the truth, not only did I complete my masters, I went ahead to Doctorate. Yes, we should rejoice over the little wins, but we must never forget what put us in motion in the first place. Until the vision is achieved, the race isn't over. Step high; aim for bigger things. Step high; refuse to remain on the spot. Step high; be everything God wants you to be.

So many of us, because of the meager resources available to us at the moment and what our present situation looks like, have given up on our big vision and made up little ones that appear more achievable. This shouldn't be the case at all because by giving up on your bigger vision in order to establish and maintain a smaller one, you are becoming something less than you might otherwise be. Besides the nature and size, your vision should not be limited to the present; let it be big and beyond the present to the extent that it is able to propel you to greater heights because if not, you are depriving yourself and the world of the real qualities and gifts you possess. With this in mind, you ought to always aim high and reach for big things regardless of your present situation or condition. You are an heir of the Almighty God, so big things are actually meant for you.

Settling for less is not a sign of humility or contentment; it is a sign of weakness, weakness to pursue, weakness to be more. Michelangelo said, "The greater danger for most of us lies in not setting our aim too high and falling short, but in setting our aim too low and achieving our mark." But Nelson Mandela said it best; "There is no passion for being found playing small – in settling for a life that is less than the one you are capable of living." Very often, we aim low because we are either not sure if our plans will come through or because our vision is limited by what other people think, what they believe, and by what their limited outlook or perception of life is. Unfortunately, most of these people are made up of individuals who have small visions and settle for less, while also living mediocre lives that do not stretch them beyond their comfort zones. In other words, they play it safe and rarely take bold actions that make them become and achieve more in life. Please don't let the perception of these small-minded people influence your desire to dream big or have a big vision because the limit of your own imagination is the only real boundary to what you are capable of doing and becoming. So, rather than aiming low, aim high and achieve greater feats. In fact, if we do not aim high, we tend to achieve very little or nothing at all. Aiming very high actually gives you substantial results, because even if you fail while aiming very high, you will still fail above so many people's low or average desire for success.

There is a common saying that goes thus: "Aim for the moon, if you miss it, you'll land among the stars." This means that when you set a high goal and you don't reach them, you'll still be able to reach something close to them. But when you aim too low, there is nothing to reach for if you miss your target. Flush out the desire to settle for little. It is a sort of restriction on your mind and the hands of God. You have already limited Him and concluded that He could not do certain things. Aiming low means that you still see some things as too big for God to answer. As a matter of fact, because your vision is like the roadmap that will guide and propel you towards achieving your God-given vision, you should have a big vision that inspires and motivates you to always aim high despite the present difficulties.

Don't build a wall around yourself. Don't set up roadblocks where they're not needed. Give your mind the freedom to explore and dream big. Spread your tentacles wide enough to reach the world by dreaming big without limits. Mediocrity is not an attribute of God; it is not an attribute we should pick up. All over the Scriptures, our God is painted as a God of excellence. His ways and thoughts are higher than those of men, and He is not limited in any way. Moreover, in keeping up with our God-given mandate to be fruitful, multiply and replenish the earth in Genesis 1:28, we often find in so many other Bible verses the call to abound or excel in our Christ-like character, especially in various ways that enable us to express love and give support to our fellow human beings. So as it is, the quest for excellence against all odds fuels our fire and keeps us from falling short of God's purpose and expectations for our lives.

The works of His hands show us how excellent He is. He is slack in nothing. He is committed to whatever He does, and He does not do the regular. This is why when we pray, He loves to exceed our expectations, and He loves to show up in ways we can't even imagine. Since our God is not a small God, then we must not be low in our thinking, we mustn't be small-minded in our aspirations; we must never think that the little things of life are sufficient for us when in the real sense, we are the owners of the bigger and better things in life.

If you miss out on God's unlimited power, it is because you have limited Him in your thoughts and plans. Many of us limit what God is planning to do through us by our small thinking and low expectations. Let off the guards around your heart and see how much of God you will experience. If only you can stretch your mind and your faith, you will be able to access all the huge gifts that God has in store for you. By trusting and believing in the hugeness of God and His unlimited capabilities, you will experience Him in ways you have never imagined, and you will be able to become all you were made to be.

MEDIOCRITY: THE GREATEST ENEMY OF SUCCESS

You know the aim is not just to do the Father's will, but to do it with all our strength and might. We strive not to be close to what we've been called to be but to be in fullness, who God designed us to be. The mediocre is okay with just being close to the fulfillment of his vision, but we cannot be satisfied until we have truly fulfilled our calling. The mediocre may be satisfied with the little achievements here and there, but we cannot be satisfied until we have accomplished the vision. I don't know about you, but I always strive to rise above mediocrity by putting in my best effort in anything I do, even when all odds are against me, I try never to settle for less bearing in mind that anything worth doing, is worth doing well.

If you look around, you will notice that many people are contented with being able to merely survive, rather than doing all they possibly can to thrive. Also, if you dare look within, you might find out that you are doing the same thing as well. Far too many of us are happy with just doing okay when we can actually push ourselves to rise above mediocrity and be the best we can ever be. I have come to realize that many people have this herd-mentality that keeps them fighting for scraps or crumbs with the "mediocre majority." Unknown to them, it is a needless fight that offers no real value even if you win. It really beats me why you will be willing to settle for less even when it is so obvious that you are capable of doing and achieving so much more. I mean God has invested a lot of great gifts in you, why allow mediocrity to hold you back from attaining your greatness. I might sound a bit clichéd but believe me; greatness doesn't come cheap; there is a hefty price to pay for it. Unfortunately, most people cannot afford to pay the price for greatness as it demands a sense of ambition and a mental capacity that never settles for mediocrity.

Remaining in the state of mediocrity will continue to sabotage your efforts until you have a reputation for being nothing but an average individual. Average has never been enough, and it never will. A lot of people only settle for it because it gives them the consolation that they are not failures

– relief that they tried. But is this really how you want to be remembered, just ok and average? In truth, your ultimate desire and drive on this earth should be to bless the world with the best of who you truly are. And of course, you cannot achieve such a great feat with an average mindset and approach to life; you must be ready not to settle for less or for almost, because even "almost" doesn't work in the kingdom business. It is either done in full measures, or it's not done at all. James 2:10 says, *"For whoever keeps the whole law and yet stumbles at just one point is guilty of breaking it all."* If it is not completely done, then it is not done at all. You have to strive to be everything that you have been called to be. Otherwise, there'd be no point.

> *"But since you're like lukewarm water, neither hot nor cold, I will spit you out of my mouth." (Revelation 3:16, NLT)*

God doesn't want you sitting on the fence because there is no place in his heavenly Kingdom for fence-sitters. He wants you to be decisive and know exactly where you belong. But why does God despise fence-sitters? It's because they are indecisive and don't really believe or trust in the greatness of God. Certainly you never really know where you stand with a fence sitter as you have no idea of knowing which way they will go since they are easily tossed to and fro depending on which direction the wind blows. I guess this is the reason why God doesn't want to have any business with a fence sitter. You can not afford to be neither here nor there because He will spit you out of His mouth according to the above Bible verse. You just have to make a firm decision to either rise above mediocrity or stay below average, and there is no in-between.

Being average is not a place to be. Those who stay there settle for anything that comes their way. They refuse to move out of their comfort zone into the place they should be. A. W. Tozer wrote: "Refuse to be average. Let your heart soar as high as it will." There is a high calling upon us, and we will never fulfill it as long as we think the average is enough. 1 Peter 2:9 tells us, *"But you are a chosen people, a royal priesthood, a holy nation, God's special possession, that you may declare the praises of Him who called you out of darkness into His wonderful light."*

Since your calling is not average, you cannot afford to be average. You are a royal priesthood, precious in the sight of God. You cannot live like an ordinary man. You are nowhere close to each other. Wake up to the reality of your calling and stop moving about in circles. To break out of the mold and eventually become limitless, you must continuously do meaningful and exceptional things that clearly set you apart from ordinary people who don't see anything wrong with remaining average.

When we become complacent about average results, we settle for a low life. When God has called you into excellence, while still dwell in mediocrity? Mediocrity is a bad attitude of laziness that makes you agree to manage whatever life throws at you. We should never settle for a life of mediocrity, yet we do;

maybe because we believe that it's easier to settle for less than going all out to face our challenges in order to make our lives better. In most cases, we are afraid of change or the failure that might occur if we take bold and daring steps. Unfortunately for us, this attitude or way of life is slowly strangling our development and progression to death because we are living a life where there is no room for significant growth. Although tackling mediocrity in your approach to life may be quite discomforting, but once you make a conscious and intentional effort to rise above mediocrity, you will begin to see mind-blowing results in your life. The only way to harness your true potential and live your life to the fullest is to stop settling for less; so raise your standards to rise above mediocrity.

Be willing to go the extra mile to get your vision accomplished. Many times, we are tempted just to manage the results that come from them. But this attitude will take us nowhere; we must be willing to try new methods to achieve the goal if the set plan does not work. Be willing to do everything within your power to bring the vision to life. There are no shortcuts to success; you have to go through the main route. Sometimes, the journey becomes elongated, but you must keep your eyes on the goal, refusing to be tempted by the small packages that lie around. So many people are so eager and in a hurry to succeed in life to the extent that they are ready to take any shortcuts that they come across. Unfortunately, these shortcuts either lead to major disappointments or small achievements rather than real and enduring success.

One of the most effective ways to deal with mediocrity is to get rid of myopic people, people who can only see little. As much as you try to aim high, these people will come up with reasons why you can't achieve it. Myopic people are dream killers who derive pleasure and satisfaction from making other people feel low about themselves. They cannot think beyond their small and myopic mindset. If this kind of people surrounds you, you need to get rid of them because they will frustrate and eventually kill your dreams. It's often said that you are the product of the people you spend most of your time with; so a man who walks in the company of fools, even if he is not a fool, will become a fool very soon. Proverbs 13:20 says, *"Walk with the wise and become wise, for a company of fools suffers harm."* Your company is very important; we get motivation or discouragement from the people who we call friends. 1 Corinthians 15:33 says, *"Do not be misled, bad company corrupts good character."*

Robert G. Allen said something profound: "Don't let the opinions of the average man sway you. Dream big, he thinks you're crazy. Succeed, and he thinks you're lucky. Acquire wealth, and he thinks you're greedy. Pay no attention. He simply doesn't understand."

Those short-sighted people don't understand why you have to chase big dreams. They don't understand why you want to leave an impact in the world after you're long gone. So they are generally hesitant or resistant to change and new ideas as they are contented with their way of life. Many of them don't even understand why you're not just satisfied with making heaven; they can't comprehend why you go through so much stress on earth just to be rewarded after death. For them, life is sweeter and better when living in a small box that is well suited for a small mindset which is locked into believing that most people will never be able to achieve great things in their life.

It doesn't have to be this way; don't be satisfied with little successes. Don't be carried away by the small packages. The vision ahead of you is a very great one. The big things will be unachievable if you allow yourself to be blinded by the small things. Don't get tired because of the hurdles you see today; they won't be there forever. Besides, the rate at which you progress in life is determined on whether or not you are willing to face your challenges with faith and hope; where an average man would quit, you as a vision-oriented individual should keep going.

WHY YOU SHOULD STEP HIGH

Step high unto greater things. After you have learned the basics, you need to move to an advanced level. This was what the Hebrew church was reminded of. *"Therefore, let us move beyond the elementary teachings about Christ and be taken forward to maturity..."* (Hebrews 6:1). There is a need to grow into expertise in your area of calling because as time goes on, much more will be expected from you.

Moreover, there is no better way to step high unto greater things than aiming to become an expert authority in your chosen field. This is so because becoming an expert in any meaningful venture requires dedication, discipline, focus, and a sincere desire to continue to push you forward no matter how hard things might get along the way. Nothing or no one should stop you from stepping high unto greater things, not even the people close to you.

Bear in mind that you are in no competition with anyone else and that you are to focus on running your own race. When you compare yourself with others, you'll end up frustrated and diverted from your journey. If there should be any comparison, it should be between who you are today and who you were yesterday. You should be able to keep track of your progress, not by comparing yourself with others but by evaluating where you are now with where you know you should be. Comparison can either make you proud or make you feel intimidated because in comparing yourself with others, you are empowering them to influence your behavior either positively or negatively. Similarly, comparing yourself with other people can sometimes be motivating and sometimes destructive; so rather than compare yourself with others, focus your energy and efforts on improving your mindset to become a better version of yourself. To do this, you must constantly check your internal scorecard in order to set personal targets that will enable you to be the benchmark of the person you want to beat. You must give yourself new heights to climb, set new records to break, create new challenges, and concentrate on being a problem solver. When you approach life with such a mindset, the only person that would be worthy of comparing yourself against is yourself, giving that the best way to achieve your own goals is to become your best self. In truth, there is only one thing you are better in doing than other people, and that is being you. There is something big in you waiting to find its full expression, and introspection is what you really need for its ultimate manifestation.

There is a great honor that comes with being the best at what you do. It opens more doors for you and gives you a wider plane of influence. It brings you before important people and places your seat among kings and influencers. The mediocre can never find a place above where he is; he cannot do well enough to attract people, talk more of blessing them with his gift.

Don't ever limit yourself. By setting a height to reach (a height you think is within your grasp), you are limiting what God can do through you. Set no constraints around yourself. As long as it is conceivable in your mind, then it is not too big to be achieved.

You need to learn to add color and life to what you do. Find better ways to do the things you've always done. Keep getting better. Give yourself room to grow and expand. As you pursue your vision, you start with the small goals and move to the bigger ones as time goes on. Start small but think and dream big, knowing that what actually makes your vision come to fruition are the intensity and magnitude of your thoughts, coupled with the positive actions that you take towards achieving them.

Often times, people forget about the main vision when they begin to achieve the small goals; they are carried away with the little achievements that they forget where they are actually headed. The small goals are supposed to lead to the main vision; they are not the stopping point. They should only inspire you to keep pursuing the vision relentlessly. They should only motivate you to take higher risks by trying new things. Forget the past glory and concentrate on the vision ahead. In truth, genuine success does not happen overnight, so it's important to commit to it by just taking small steps that are carefully calculated and well thought out at targeted intervals. If you study the biographies of successful people like Bill Gates, Jeff Bezos, Elon Musk, Aliko Dangote, Tony Elumelu, etc., you will see that they started from the bottom to build to the top. Even though they all had big dreams, they all started small because they understood that success like most things in life is a journey; and that the only way to fulfill this journey is to take small steps that will collectively and eventually amount to meaningful steps that helps pull you closer and closer to your desired destination. Therefore, you should only use small achievements as stepping stones on your journey towards achieving bigger and better things in life.

Having said that, beware of over-celebrating your small achievements while being spotlighted on stage. Also, don't get carried away or overly excited by those clapping for you while you are on stage; the thunderous clapping of their hands is a loud ovation that can easily make you lose sight of the bigger picture and vision. As a matter of fact, it is when you sense that you are actually performing at your peak that you should go all out to step up your performance levels in order to keep achieving more successes from one stage to another. This mindset explains why most electronic products today keep getting updated; before you are able to understand the functionality of the devices fully, another model is released. It is a product you will want to have simply because the manufacturer has added a feature which they have discovered entices the majority of their customers. What do you have to offer that is new? What is the new invention from your vision? Innovation is the birthplace of ovation. Don't settle for that small achievement, that little breakthrough, that modest promotion, press forward to achieve more.

Paul said in Philippians 3:14: *"I press on toward the goal to win the prize for which God has called me heavenward in Christ Jesus."*

Let your eyes remain fixed on the goal. There is an expected end God wants you to reach, and until you get there, there is no prize for you. If you want to claim this prize, then you will have your eyes fixed on the goal and become oblivious to the distractions around you. They are planted there by the enemy to make you lose focus. Mind you; these distractions can be positive or negative. What are distractions? They are side attractions, different from your assignment but begging for your attention. They are traps of the enemy to make you deviate from your vision. But glory to God, we are not ignorant of the devices of the devil. I pray that God will give you the spirit of discernment to know when the enemy applies subtle but dangerous tricks that can destroy your vision. Mind your calling, focus on your assignment, and your mind will be sound and you will be able to identify any distraction.

When Jesus performed the first miracle of turning water into wine, He could have chosen to relax and enjoy the honor accorded Him as the miracle worker. But He didn't. If He had, He would have been alienated from fulfilling the main purpose of being on earth – to save man. Lay the awards and commendations from people aside and keep your eyes focused on the vision.

As good as appraisals are, they can blind you and stand as a stumbling block for you on the road to success. Accept them, embrace them but let them not be the reason why the bigger vision slips off your hands. Self-appraisal is the best kind of appraisal because you will appraise yourself based on the vision and picture of the future you have seen. As I fondly say, if you are not ready to move to the next level, the position you are currently occupying is another person's prayer point, and God will answer them. It is your choice to move upward and allow others to rise. That's why when you sit on a seat for too long; it becomes a hot seat.

Step high. Become the best at what you do, oh yes! Aim to become the best of the best. Break your own records, break other people's records and keep setting the pace, you are a city that is set on a hill, you are ordained to be only above, not beneath. Bishop David Oyedepo once said God told him, "My son, there is a place for you on top if you are interested." What God says to one, He says to all. One thing that drives me is the picture of the future I see and the magnificent view of my place at the top.

Step high; this is not the time to relax, but the time to take possession and ownership of your own place at the top. Be excellence-driven; think of better ways, and aim higher than where you are. Step up!

CHAPTER SIX

STEP BACK FOR A STEP UP

Step back for a step up. Sounds awkward? But this is not what you think; the step back here does not imply taking steps backward; it means you are looking for a time and moment to reflect and refresh for another leap. Although everything about always moving or stepping forward in life offers a positive and incremental perception that makes forward or onward movements worthy of pursuing all the time, you must know that it's also important for you to step back sometimes in order to review and reevaluate the progress you have made so far. In short, sometimes you have to take a couple of steps back to move forward again in the right direction. There are things you may never see inside your God-given vision, so sometimes you will need to step out of the 'vision' to relate with the Creator who gave you the vision in the first place. You will need that moment to go back to the manufacturer for overhauling, maintenance and reassurance. This is what propels us to higher ground and ultimately a step up in our purpose and vision.

How does stepping back propel you to higher ground?

After long strenuous months of work, there always comes that time to relax and re-energize for a new beginning.

Vacation is a season everyone looks forward to because we get the privilege to wash off all the stress and make new plans. This is why students go on vacation, workers go on leave, and churches go on retreats. It is for a purpose: to relax and re-energize.

There also comes that time when masters step back for their protégés to take the space. After months of tutelage, the master steps aside for his apprentice to have the floor. In this way, their knowledge is tested, and they gain experience, which will eventually increase the output of the master directly or indirectly.

When the apostles began the work of the ministry by preaching the gospel everywhere they went, they started based on Jesus' command. All they needed to do was heed the call and carry out the assignment. When it was time for conversion, they allowed the Holy Spirit to convince them and make them believe the message. They left it for the Spirit to do. As they laid their hands on people, they didn't do it with confidence in themselves. They only obeyed and stepped aside for God to do the Job.

Yes, you have yielded to the prompting in you. You have started running the race you were commissioned to do. You have a set down vision, and you are already working with it. While this is good, there is a time when you need to step aside and allow God to breathe in what you do. There is a time when you need to step aside for God to take over.

There are three dimensions to stepping back. The first is that you step back to recharge and re-strategize. The second is that you step back for your protégés to do the work while the last is that you step back, take your hands off and let God take over. When you let go of your strength and wisdom, God has a free course in your life. If you want a step up, then you have to step aside for God to take control. You also need to have a moment of relaxation and reflection.

STEP BACK TO RECHARGE AND RE-STRATEGIZE

As you pursue your vision, there is a need for a period when you pull away from activities to catch your breath, evaluate yourself to know exactly how you should continue on the journey. You need to step back so that you can step up. It really pays to take a break in order to move forward because taking a step back to review your present situation or condition can help you clarify why your current approach isn't working well enough and what you should do to progress better in life. Taking such breaks will help you clearly see where you are in your life's journey, how you need to proceed next, and how to leverage your progress in the past to achieve better results in the future. This will give you more zeal and confidence to make more meaningful and purposeful strides in your life's journey. As you know, the journey to the fulfillment of purpose is not a day's journey; it is a journey of so many years. For some, it takes their entire lifetime, for some others, it takes a lesser time;

but no matter how long, it is impossible to keep going for years without taking a moment to rest and assess your progress.

When you step back, you hibernate to restart again. You go back to recharge and come out stronger. By the time you resume, you begin to operate on a higher level and with greater influence. So as it is, the time invested in taking a step or several steps backward to reflect and refresh is not wasted at all. Sometimes you need to take one step backward to propel yourself two steps forward. Greatness is like a spring; you take a step back to keep springing forth.

The step back period is the season of rest; a pause to continue later. It is not an abrupt end to the pursuit of purpose. It doesn't come when the vision is still young; instead, it comes when it is already gaining major momentum, and a few days off duty will do no harm. Whether the plan has been coming through or not, you need the step back to evaluate yourself and see how far you have come. You need it to assess the areas where you have been doing well and those where you need to put in more effort. The step back period is a self-evaluation and introspection that helps you know what works and what doesn't; it helps you to audit your life both internally and externally to the point of improving your performance in many areas or aspects of life. Whether you realize it or not, implementing a step back review process that involves self-evaluation and self-introspection at targeted intervals of your life's journey is essential to your personal, professional and spiritual growth. So it actually pays to intentionally set time aside for a step back review and reflection of all the steps you have taken thus far.

When doing this, you have to be true and sincere with yourself so that you can measure your progress. Don't magnify little things or make little of big things. See things as they really are so you can take note of the areas that need to be worked upon. Take note of your mistakes and what led to them so that you can avoid them in the future. Mistakes should not weigh us down; instead, they should be lessons for us to learn from and not dwell on negatively or regretfully. In truth, how we respond and learn from mistakes or challenges helps to define who we are in the long run.

So when stepping back, do so to learn new skills and make new plans for a better phase of your life's journey. Maximize the period by learning new skills relevant to your journey. Acquire knowledge by reading and learning from experts in your field. When you begin to input the newly gathered information in your work, there will be a greater difference and much more results. As a matter of fact, this new perspective allows you to fine-tune your own plans and avoid certain pitfalls by so doing.

It is important that you set apart time for personal development. What new qualities do you need to adopt? What do you lack? Use this period to develop qualities such as discipline, consistency, punctuality, and any other positive quality that may be absent in you. Practice these qualities with the little things around you. For discipline, practice restricting yourself from taking certain things you love but are harmful to you. Set a time to wake up and a time to get something important done. For consistency, practice doing the same thing over and over again, even if it is a fun-filled activity. Just make sure that you become a better version of yourself before launching out again. By the time you launch out again, you must be able to identify new qualities you were able to adopt.

You can go for a fast, which will help your Spirit to reconnect back to its source, make your mind sober and supercharged; cleanse your body of all residues. Fasting brings emotional peace and strength, and it revitalizes the body.

STEP BACK FOR OTHERS TO STEP IN

The true definition of leadership is being able to replicate yourself in other people. A true leader births other leaders. It is not enough to have people to submit to you and learn from you. You must give them a platform through which they can give expression to the knowledge gained over time. If you have people who work with you, it is also important that you step back and give them a chance to do some of the things you'd do ordinarily. Allow them to make mistakes and get better; while it may seem like a risky thing to do, elevating your impact as a leader requires you to embrace the spirit of delegation because it empowers your subordinates by giving them a chance to step up and prove their worth in the grand scheme of things. Let them get a chance to influence others as well, this will surely open you up to other new and considerable ways of doing meaningful things towards the fulfillment of your purpose in life.

Jesus laid down this example for us in the training of the disciples. After He performed series of teaching and miracles, he sent them on a mission. Even though He knew they weren't mature yet and were susceptible to mistakes, He sent them out anyway. How would they gain experience if they didn't practice?

> *"When Jesus had called the Twelve together, He gave them power and authority to drive out all demons and to cure diseases, and He sent them out to proclaim the kingdom of God and to heal the sick." (Luke 9:1-2).*

Like Jesus, we also should be able to train people, nurture them in their gifts and allow them to express themselves. We should be able to produce ourselves in other people; people who can do the things we do and even more. Jesus said in John 14:12, *"Whoever believes in me will do the works I have been doing, and they will do even greater things than these."* Jesus produced others like himself, and He expects that we should be able to reproduce ourselves in other people.

Having groomed these people, there should be times when we leave the space and let them have the show. While they are getting better themselves, these people will help increase our plane of influence and will be able to reach people and places we may never reach – isn't this a step up for us?

Be committed to a formidable strategy that will help you to identify and grow future leaders in your plan to bring your vision to fruition, knowing that the greatness and fulfillment of your purpose lie in your ability to produce successors that will keep carrying and passing your torch of success. In other words, you must be able to transfer your experience and expertise for your legacy and that of those within your circle of influence to continue to live on. Abraham raised Isaac; Moses steps back for Joshua; David did not only train his son Solomon but also prepared the materials for him to succeed.

STEP BACK FOR GOD TO TAKE OVER

As humans, there is a limit to how far our wisdom and strength can take us in life. This is why we must learn to lean on God. After playing our parts as humans by yielding to God's call, we must learn to step back and let God bless our works. 1 Corinthians 3:7 (NKJV) says, *"So then neither he who plants is anything, nor he who waters, but only God who gives the increase."* This means that no matter what we do and how much we do it, God is the One who blesses it and gives increases.

"Trust in the Lord with all your heart, and lean not on your own understanding. In all your ways acknowledge Him, and He will direct your path." Proverbs 3:5-6

You need the pause to seek God's direction and know where He'd have you go. Understand where your power as a man ends; invite God to help you in your weakness. Set apart some time to be with the Lord, because He is the source of your inspiration. Take some time off, blessing the crowd in order to be blessed by God. Have a set time to rebuild yourself and get new words and instructions from God. When you do this, you will see an obvious transformation on your journey to the fulfillment of purpose.

Stepping back is one of the most powerful secrets anyone who wants to succeed must know. You cannot be at the forefront every time; there are times when you need to pull out into your closet speaking to the Lord and gathering more capacity for the greater tasks ahead. As you continue to aim higher and higher in life, a host of predicaments will confront you on your way up. These predicaments can quickly escalate into disastrous experiences that keep you stuck in a place of fear and despair unless you have a godly perspective that helps you know when it's time to let go and let God. Our Creator has the supernatural ability to replace our earthly worries with heavenly blessings, so it is wise for us to know when to step back in order to allow him to take charge of our predicaments and turn our unwanted situations into awe-inspiring outcomes. If you fail to let go and let God when you ought to, you won't be able to gather enough strength for the responsibility ahead of you, and you will fail eventually. This was why the angel of God told Elijah to eat well enough for the journey ahead of Him. *"And the angel of the Lord came again the second time, and touched him, and said, 'Arise and eat; because the journey is too great for you."* (1 Kings 19:7, NKJV)

Trust God to lead you every step of the way. Know when to retreat. Submit to Him. Step back for Him to lift you up. Take life God's way instead of your own way; don't be so carried away by the vision that you leave out the giver of the vision. Whenever you step back to be still and quiet with a fixed gaze waiting on the Lord for his direction, you will certainly feel his close presence, and your worries will eventually be settled. So ensure you always make out time to wait upon the Lord because he is the source where all your strength comes from. Isaiah 40:31 (NKJ) says, *"But those who wait on the Lord shall renew their strength; they shall mount up with wings like eagles, they shall run and not be weary, they shall walk and not faint."*

Step back and let HIM be God Almighty in your life!

CHAPTER SEVEN

STEP FORWARD FOR A STEP UP

The major reason why fulfilling God's purpose seems unachievable for some people is that they fail to take up opportunities. They lack the boldness to step forward and seize the opportunities around them. Positioning yourself to be able to take advantage of as many opportunities as possible is very important because oftentimes one of these opportunities can mean the difference between having a purposeful life and having a mediocre one that is uneventful. God has placed many opportunities around us, but many times, we fail to tap into them. Opportunities are given to be harnessed, but when they're not, they just waste away. Time waits for no one; an opportunity missed may never be regained.

"Making the most of your time because the days are evil."
(Ephesians 5:16, NASB)

You need to learn to take advantage of the opportunities littered around you; these opportunities lie in resources, in people, and connections, everywhere around us. Unfortunately, most of us miss out on leveraging opportunities due to the fact that we are either ill-prepared or so distracted with other life issues that we miss the majority of the opportunity that comes our way. Thomas Edison had a slightly different viewpoint when he said; "Most people miss opportunity because it is dressed in overalls and looks like work." In any case, don't miss out on your opportunities because of lack of preparation, laziness to work, and unnecessary distractions. God has placed these opportunities around you to make the journey easier. When we fail to harness them, we make fulfilling purpose unnecessarily difficult for ourselves.

Never be afraid to step forward and claim opportunities near you. Understandably, you might have tried things that failed in the past, which might have formed a restriction around you that makes it hard to seize opportunities. You need to stop living in the past because one of the keys to stepping forward into the future we envision and pray about is to forget the past. Take progressive steps and not regressive ones. Step forward and not backward. Live in the present by harnessing all the privileges around you today. I know this seems like a contradiction to my earlier chapter on stepping back to move forward, but by forgetting the past, I mean that you should not allow your past to interfere with the present to the extent that it robs you of your future. The truth be told, there is a lot of value in reflecting on the past so that we can learn and grow from it, but as you do this, you should not be consumed or controlled by the past, and then be defined by it. Keep on gravitating to what lies ahead and onwards by seeing, sensing and seizing the opportunities around you.

Nehemiah is one of the Bible characters who were very smart about seizing the opportunity around them. Standing before the king with wine to serve, Nehemiah wasted no time in making his request known, and immediately the king showed concern about his sad countenance.

"In the month of Nisan in the twentieth year of King Artaxerxes, when wine was brought before him, I took the wine and gave it to the king. I had not been sad in his presence before, so the king asked me, 'Why do you look so sad when you are not ill? This can be nothing but sadness of heart.' But I said to the king, 'May the king live forever! Why should my face not look sad when the city where my ancestors are buried lies in ruins and its gates have been destroyed by fire?' The king said to me, 'What is it you want?' And I answered the king, 'If it pleases the king and if your servant has found favor in his sight, let him send me to the city in Judah, where my ancestors are buried so that I can rebuild it.' Then the king, with the queen sitting beside him, asked me, 'How long will your journey take? And when will you get back? It pleased the king to send me, so I set a time. I also said to him, 'If it pleases the king, may I have letters to the governors of Trans-Euphrates so that they will provide me safe-conduct until I arrive Judah? And may I have a letter to Asaph, keeper of the royal park, so he will give me timber to make beams

for the gates of the citadel by the temple and for the city wall and for the residence I will occupy?' And because the gracious hand of my God was on me, the king granted my requests." – Nehemiah 2:1-8

For some of us, our response to the king's question would have been, "I'm fine. I'm just a little tired." By pretending to be strong, we miss opportunities clearly prepared by God. There was no iota of delay in his response to the king. He did not even hold back anything. He asked the king for everything that he knew he could give. He took advantage of the privilege to bring the burden in his heart to life. We can step up in the actualization of our vision when we step forward to seize opportunities like Nehemiah. He had wished a day like that would come; immediately, the king showed concern; he just kept pouring out his heart.

God had laid the vision of rebuilding the walls of Jerusalem in his heart, and of course, he had lacked the resources and freedom to go and carry it out. The only thing he did was get himself prepared to seize the opportunity when it came. If you want to save yourself the stress of working hard for everything, you need to step forward and seize opportunities around you. A man who knows how to seize opportunities will walk at a faster pace than a man who doesn't. God does not want us to struggle; He basically needs us to obey. This is why He provides opportunities around us. Unfortunately, many of us are not even sensitive enough to see these opportunities.

When blind Bartimaeus heard that Jesus Christ was passing by, he kept shouting until he attracted the attention of Jesus. He didn't see; he only heard that the great miracle worker was around, and he seized the opportunity to get his healing. Jesus didn't see him, but he didn't stop calling Jesus until he was ministered to. How many of us are like Bartimaeus who understood how to get what he wanted? He even knew how to invite the opportunity to himself.

> *"Then they came to Jericho. As Jesus and his disciples, together with a large crowd, were leaving the city, a blind man, Bartimaeus (which means "son of Timaeus"), was sitting by the roadside begging. When he heard that it was Jesus of Nazareth, he began to shout, "Jesus, Son of David, have mercy on me!" Many rebuked him and told him to be quiet, but he shouted all the more, "Son of David, have mercy on me!" Jesus stopped and said, "Call him." So they called to the blind man, "Cheer up! On your feet! He's calling you." Throwing his cloak aside, he jumped to his feet and came to Jesus. "What do you want me to do for you?" Jesus asked him. The blind man said, "Rabbi, I want to see." "Go," said Jesus, "your faith has healed you." Immediately he received his sight and followed Jesus along the road." – Mark 10:46-52*

Esther also took advantage of her position as the queen to save her fellow Jews. When Haman received the order from the king to kill the Jews, Mordecai urged her to go before the king and speak to him. It was wrong to appear before the king uninvited, but she went anyway after praying and fasting for three days. After prayers, the next thing she did was take action. She stepped forward by leveraging on her position and pre-offered prayers. And God did not fail her; the king granted her request.

"Esther again pleaded with the king, falling at his feet and weeping. She begged him to put an end to the evil plan of Haman the Agagite, which he had devised against the Jews. Then the king extended the gold scepter to Esther, and she arose and stood before him. "If it pleases the king," she said, "and if he regards me with favor and thinks it the right thing to do, and if he is pleased with me, let an order be written overruling the dispatches that Haman son of Hammedatha, the Agagite, devised and wrote to destroy the Jews in all the king's provinces. For how can I bear to see disaster fall on my people? How can I bear to see the destruction of my family?" King Xerxes replied to Queen Esther and to Mordecai the Jew, "Because Haman attacked the Jews, I have given his estate to Esther, and they have impaled him on the pole he set up. Now write another decree in the king's name in behalf of the Jews as seems best to you, and seal it with the king's signet ring—for no document written in the king's name and sealed with his ring can be revoked." – Esther 8:3-8

Opportunities don't last forever. You have to grab them as they come. One opportunity may be your propelling force into the actualization of the vision. Learning to take opportunities begins with learning to say "yes" to special responsibilities and privileges when they show up. When someone is needed to do something you can do, make yourself available. This is very important because pushing yourself out of your comfort zone to take on more responsibility is a great way to grow personally, professionally, and spiritually. You never can tell who will be watching and be willing to help you step up to greater heights. Besides, suppose it is what you are called to do or in an area. In that case, you are familiar with, you should always be open to finding more opportunities to keep serving in that capacity as this will eventually make you a person of great value. So never fail to bless the people around you with your gift and calling, and don't hesitate to embrace new opportunities as they come your way.

You need to learn to take more risks because knowing the risks to take, and how to take them can be extremely useful and helpful in stacking the odds in your favor. Besides, life is about taking risks, and if you never take risks, you might never be able to achieve your dreams or do great things because there is really no way of knowing what you are capable of if you don't take risks in life. The greatest opportunities usually have the greatest risks. If you want to know how to maximize opportunities, then you need to know how to take risks. When taking a risk, do it with a positive mindset. It helps you believe in possibilities and makes your mind clear enough to find a way in the clumsiest place.

You should also have a passion to know. There are so many opportunities that have eluded us because we didn't even know about it. As a person who wants to be fulfilled, you must have a burning desire for knowledge. This is so because knowledge is central to developing the ability to be successful in any of your chosen fields. Without deep knowledge, it may be difficult to recognize opportunities when they come. In your quest to know more, you will find new ideas and new opportunities that you can maximize to become who you were made to be.

Make new friends. Connect with new people. By increasing your connections, you are opening yourself up to more opportunities because opportunities lie in people. Opportunities come mostly through people you know and not necessarily the things you know. As a matter of fact, the opportunities that the act of true friendship provides far outweigh anything that can be found in other possessions. So it is wise to use a great fervor and positive energy in pursuing connections with new people that can add real value to your life as this feat will help to increase the number of opportunities that you access. I mean if you really think about it, what is a vision without people.

Focus on that very thing you want in life and put all your energy into it. Become the best at it and improve on self-development. Opportunities are more effective when they meet with preparation. This is why the most focused and prepared people are the ones who make the most of opportunities. When you have a single focus that you are adequately prepared for, you are able to develop yourself in that specific area and are also able to position yourself for the opportunities in that field. I really like and appreciate the Boy Scout's motto which simply admonishes its members to "Be Prepared" at all times because it clearly reflects and represents the need to constantly and consistently be in a state of readiness in your mind and body in order to be able to perform whatever duty is necessary towards contributing to the attainment of a better society and finding your own fulfillment in life as well. When in any given situation you are prepared, it means that you are internally ready and physically fit to perform as need be. In short, preparation is one of the most important aspects of life when it comes to succeeding in your chosen field, as well as in uncovering and fulfilling your purpose. A good way to sum this up is with a quote by Bobby Unser, which says: "Success is where preparation and opportunity meets."

It is also important that you give yourself to prayer and develop your spirit for discernment. You must know the opportunities to take and those to run away from because finding lasting success is largely dependent on choosing the right opportunities that align well with your vision and purpose in life. Not all opportunities are really opportunities; some are traps. Proverbs 14:12 says, *"There is a way that appears to be right, but in the end, it leads to death."* You need to be able to discern between opportunities and traps, so you don't end up in regrets. If you pray well and give yourself to the Spirit's leading, you'll be saved from making such terrible mistakes. God does not want us falling in and out of error. This is why we have His Spirit to lead us every day as we go.

Great things are just around the corner for you. You need to step forward to see them. You need to take a leap of faith before you can grab it. All the people who have enjoyed transforming opportunities did not fold their arms, sit at home, and wait for an opportunity to stroll by. No. they get up, step forward and grab all the right opportunities. You should also develop this attitude in life. Life demands that you live daily with a sense of urgency that will motivate and propel you to steadily progress until you get to your desired destination based on God's purpose for your life. You cannot be complacent about life and expect to have the results of those who are very intentional about their lives. All God wants and expects from you is to be ready and prepared to take advantage of the right opportunities, knowing that his plans for you are continually open doors for you as you, in turn, continue to move forward and onward towards fulfilling your purpose in life.

Do you want to step up? C'mon, take a step forward and keep pushing. Be bold and adventurous; make a move right now and step forward for a step up in destiny.

A LIFE WELL LIVED

A life well-lived is a life that fulfills God's intent. A life lived according to God's intent is one that fulfills the purpose for which it was made. No matter how great the accomplishments may seem, if that life does not come into the full expression of why it was made, then it has not fulfilled the Father's intent. On the last day, we will be judged based on how we lived our lives here? Did we live for God, or we went about pursuing our desires? Did we live according to God's purpose, or we lived our self-made purpose?

The only thing that will matter after all is said and done is whether we lived as God intended or not. We will be held accountable for the talents and resources invested in us to carry out our assignment. The money will not matter. Fame will fade away. The assets will have no place. It will just be you before your creator giving an account of how you lived your life? What would you rather you tell Him?

Will you tell Him the number of cars you drove or the number of children you had? Will you tell Him of how men that hailed you as you walked? Definitely not; instead you will give an account of how you maximized your gifts and spent all the years you were given on earth. If you have come this far, but you cannot confidently say that you are walking on purpose, then you have to take a pause and redirect your life.

A few pounds every thirty days will not give you the fulfillment your heart yearns for; it won't earn you God's reward. All that you work for on earth ends here on earth. It is the only service to God that transcends time. The only things that'll always stand are works done in the Lord and for the Lord. Everything else will fade away. When put through the fire, your works will not stand the test of time because they are not founded in God.

Make a decision today to live your life fully for God-your maker. The life lived well is one that is lived for God.

Make out time for God. Build a relationship with Him so that you are not merely working for Him but also walking with Him. This is the reason why Christ came - to restore man's relationship with God. We must make good use of this grace so that we can be all that God wants us to be.

We will never fully know ourselves if we don't build a beautiful relationship with God. He has chosen us before the foundation of the world and knows us more than anyone else will ever do. Keep your relationship with God ablaze all through the journey to the place of destiny. Do not rate the assignment above the giver of the assignment. Beyond the discovery of purpose, you will need guidance as you pursue the vision. When you detach yourself from God, you detach yourself from life.

The vision becomes an ambition when God is no longer involved in it. The aim is no longer to glorify God but to make a name for yourself. God does not have a hand in this. Let your service be to God and not for the sake of money, accumulation of possession or fame. Matthew 6:24 (NLV) says, "*No one can serve two masters. For you will hate one and love the other; you will be devoted to one and despise the other. You cannot serve God and be enslaved to money.*"

If your vision is sponsored by a desire to have the things of the world, there is a risk of being denied the blessings of fulfillment, and ultimately, there shall be no reward for you. Let love for God and the expansion of His Kingdom become your major drive. Love for the things of the world shows that you do not really love the Lord. 1 John 2:15 (NLV) tells us, "*Do not love this world nor the things it offers you, for when you love the world, you do not have a love of the Father in you.*"

Love God with all your heart and might. When you love God, you'll value fellowship with Him and be willing to obey His instructions. Love for God will propel you to do His will and stay true to Him. Love will help you to stay focus and you will be able to say no to worldly advertisements that may want to steal away your commitment to God. Let God's love fill your heart and mind.

"Teacher, which is the greatest commandment in the Law?" And He said to him, "You shall love the Lord your God with all your heart and with all your soul and with all your mind. This is the great and first commandment."
– *Matthew 22:36-38(ESV)*

Give yourself to the knowledge of God. As you get to know Him more, you can better harness His promises for a fruitful journey. The more you know the Lord, the deeper your convictions grow in Him. Our convictions matter a lot in our walk with God. The reason why God stops making sense to you is probably because you never had convictions about Him in the first place. You have to fellowship with God and His Word. Let it transform you and keep you grounded in God.

Be sure that your vision is on the right foundation. Be in fellowship with God. A branch that separates itself from the main tree will be denied of nutrients and in no time, will wither. When you fail to fellowship with God, you deny Him as your essence and become unable to enjoy life in Him. In all that you do, be sure that you bring glory to God. Let God be your driving force.

"So whether you eat or drink or whatever you do, do it all for the glory of God." - 1 Corinthians 10:31

You are called for a purpose; gifted for a reason; blessed to be a blessing. Don't stop living for that purpose. In the end, it will be the only thing that matters.

Moreover, if you really believe that it is only God that can give you a fulfilled life, but you are yet to have an intimate relationship with him, here is a '**prayer of salvation**' that can help you experience everlasting intimacy with God:

"*Heavenly Father, I recognize that I'm a sinner, and I ask for your forgiveness for my sins. I confess in my heart and with my mouth that Jesus Christ is your Son who died on the cross for all my sins. I believe that Christ did all that will ever be necessary for me to dwell in your holy presence forever. I thank you that Christ was raised from the dead as a guarantee of my own eternal life. As best as I can, I now accept Jesus Christ as my personal Lord and savior, and I praise you for making this way for me. Please come into my life and continue to fill my heart with your Holy Spirit. Help me to trust you, help me to love you, and help me to live for you. I thank you for the new creation you have made me – in Jesus' name, amen.*"

If indeed you prayed this prayer with your heart, you are now saved and ready to start *Living As God Intended*... Congratulations!

ACKNOWLEDGEMENT

One sure thing I've realized over the years is that I am a product of grace and I owe everything about my life to God, my Father, and my Creator, who designed and crafted me for His purpose and in honor of His glory.

Having said this, I am particularly thankful:

To my wife – my sweetie and best friend, and my Children; Favor, Flourish, and Faith for the patient and encouraging love I have received from them through the years of fulfilling God's plan and purpose for my life. I love you all!

To my biological parents, the Reverend and Pastor Mrs. Abednego Odin, who raised me to know God and trust Him with my destiny; thanks for always praying for me.

To Rev E.T Omole of blessed memories for encouraging and stirring up my spirit to seek God in order to locate my vision in life.

To my prophet, my teacher and father in the Lord, Dr. David Oyedepo - through whose light I see greater light. I'm forever grateful, Sir.

To my mentor, Bishop David Abioye – for showing me what it means to be a faithful servant to my maker, and also to Pastor David Oyedepo Jnr (PDO) – who saw something in me and constantly guided me with words of wisdom and instructions that constructed me.

To everyone who helped in one way or another in the design and publication of this book, Lauretta Chinenye, Chuma Obum, and their team members. I am forever grateful, thank you.

To Glyn, and Glyness who stood by me in my seasons of test and early days of pursuing a purpose-driven life as God intended. I will forever appreciate that Bible you brought to me when I needed one to study alone with God.

To WMA – WCI members of staff who in one way or the other have helped me to know myself better and improve myself to become a better people person.

The list is endless, but also I want to especially thank members of my congregation, as well as readers of this book, for being part of my destiny and helping this dream come to life. God bless you richly; together, we will fulfill God's plans and purpose without failure in Jesus' name.

ABOUT THE AUTHOR

For over two decades, Nathaniel Odin has been in ministry primarily called to raise destinies, give hope to the hopeless and empower people to live a better life.

He believes strongly in living life to the fullest as God intended, this he further demonstrates in his dogged approach in coaching and mentoring. He possesses a wealth of experience in business mentoring, which was his background before answering the call to full-time pastoring; he is a lecturer, a trainer, and a philanthropist.

Nathaniel renders his Pastoral stewardship under his spiritual father and mentor's leadership, Dr. David Oyedepo, the president and presiding Bishop of Living Faith Church Worldwide Inc.

He currently serves as the National pastor to the church network in Europe and by privilege the Resident Pastor of Winners Chapel International, London, where he leads a congregation of over 6,000 members.

He is happily married to Mandy, and they are blessed with three Children – Favor, Flourish, and Faith.

Printed in Great Britain
by Amazon

35955122R00067